Masters
of cinema

Federico
Fellini

CAHIERS DU
CINEMA

Àngel Quintana

Contents

5   **Introduction**

7   **The post-war years**
Popular culture and neo-realism

15 **Beyond neo-realism**
From *Variety Lights* to *Nights of Cabiria*

37 **After the economic miracle**
From *La Dolce Vita* to *Amarcord*

73 **Confronting the neo-television empire**
From *Fellini's Casanova* to *La voce della luna*

96 Chronology

98 Filmography

100 Selected Bibliography

Marcello Mastroianni and Anita Ekberg in *La Dolce Vita* (1960).

Introduction

Who was Federico Fellini? When he died, on 31 October 1993, he was hailed by the media as a unique *auteur* from a golden age of Italian cinema, now long gone. For many film buffs, however, Fellini had earned his place in history as the creator of an exuberant baroque world and as the source of an adjective — Felliniesque — that has now passed into common parlance.

Fellini was a very popular filmmaker who won four Oscars (for *La strada*, *Nights of Cabiria*, *8½* and *Amarcord*). He cut his teeth in the neo-realism of the 1940s by co-scripting two milestones of film history: Roberto Rossellini's *Rome, Open City* and *Paisan*. In the 1950s some critics accused him of being moralistic, while in the following decade, when he delved into the malaise of modern society, he was considered the *auteur par excellence*. In the 1970s, *Amarcord* brought him extraordinary popularity and, finally, in the 1980s he became a lone quixotic figure in an age of empty cinemas, fighting against the empire of neo-television[1] that sprung from the mushrooming of private channels. In his journey from neo-realism to neo-television, from *The White Sheik* to *La voce della luna*, Fellini tried out different ways of looking at the world and exploring the many layers of reality surrounding the society of spectacle.

Fellini's greatest contribution to modernity was undoubtedly his insistence on making the examination of his own work the substance of his style. By honing in on the illusion of spectacle and reflecting on the faultlines of creation, many of his films deal with the creative process itself and put the *auteur* at their very heart. Fellini adopted a number of *alter egos* to set up a complex game of mirrors that used his own dreams, memories, desires, frustrations and obsessions to investigate the way our modern reality is constructed.

Federico Fellini in the 1950s.

The post-war years

Popular culture and neo-realism

Federico Fellini in the 1950s.

Right: Federico Fellini and Anna Magnani
in Robert Rossellini's 'Il miracolo' (1948).

Confluence of viewpoints

In 1948 Roberto Rossellini shot 'Il miracolo', the first segment of his anthology film *L'amore*. Its main character is Nanni, a poor, simple-minded shepherdess, played by Anna Magnani. She is seduced by a tramp, whom she takes for a messenger from God. The rogue makes her pregnant and she believes she is bearing a divine seed; she is rejected by the villagers — even by the idiots, who regard her as mad rather than a saint. The film is distinguished by its fascinating intertwining of viewpoints: that of the objective gaze — the camera — and the subjective gaze — the character. While the camera does not seek to demonstrate anything but merely records the profound ambiguity of reality, the character's viewpoint is steeped in hallucination. Nanni believes that she has been chosen to bring the Holy Spirit into the world. The confluence of these two viewpoints allows Rossellini to reflect on the difficult coexistence of material reality and a spiritual reality imbued with mystery.

The actor playing the part of the tramp was the film's scriptwriter, Federico Fellini. His presence goes beyond mere anecdotal interest, as 'Il miracolo' was made at a time when the foundations of cinematic modernity were being laid. On the one hand, the film anticipates the journey Rossellini would embark upon with *Stromboli* (1950), where he explored the idea of 'revelation': by this he meant dealing with the spiritual understanding of mystery in a way that would enable cinema to expose a reality far more complex than that of surface appearances. On the other hand, 'Il miracolo' also seems to sketch out the path that would be followed by Fellini throughout his career, as it explores the way in which a personal viewpoint can transcend reality to enter into strange hallucinatory worlds.

So, Fellini was initiated in neo-realism, just after World War II — a time characterized by a heightened awareness of the effect of the real.[2] His work spans five decades, during which he never ceased to ask questions about the representation of reality. Under the auspices of Rossellini, he discovered that social reality can veer off into delirium if problems connected with the construction of identity are not tackled. Fellini's deluded visionaries and simpletons became the projections of a theme — identity as the main factor determining reality — that emerged in post-war Italy, passed through the pipe dreams of the economic miracle and ended up entangled in the triumphant society of the spectacle. Dream, memory, desire and spectacle nourish a

Three drawings by Federico Fellini.

child's unconscious and remain a significant force in adulthood. Fellini captures this process on film by making his characters extensions of an ego nostalgic for the ephemeral but yearning for permanence.

Fellini was twenty-eight years old when he played the part of the tramp in 'Il miracolo' but he was was already relatively well known in the film business because he had worked as a co-screenwriter with big names in Italian cinema such as Roberto Rossellini, Alberto Lattuada and Pietro Germi. He had gorged himself on the cultural phenomena of the time: comic strips, caricatures, variety theatre and radio. He had worked in all these fields and, although he wound up in cinema (starting as a creator of gags for popular comedies), they would, along with the circus, prove the main fulcrums for his cinematic style.

Caricatures and variety

Federico Fellini was born in Rimini on 20 January 1920. It was there that he spent his childhood and lived through the dark years of Fascism. The eldest son of Urbano Fellini, a commercial salesman, and Ida Barbiani, Federico had one brother, Riccardo (1921−91), and one sister, Maddalena (1929−2004). He was crazy about *fumetti* (comic strips), especially the ones that appeared in *Il Corriere dei Piccoli*; his imagination was fired by characters such as Mickey Mouse, Mandrake the Magician, Flash Gordon, Felix the Cat and Buck Rogers. In 1937 he drew a series of caricatures of famous actors for the Fulgor cinema in Rimini and, the following year, the newspaper *La*

Domenica del Corriere published his first cartoons. In 1939 he moved to Rome with his mother and sister, and once there he lived from his drawing for the first few years. He joined the staff of *Marc'Aurelio*, a successful twice-weekly humorous political magazine published by Rizzoli. In 1944, after the liberation of Rome on 4 June, he joined forces with some draughtsmen colleagues to open the Funny Face Shop, which thrived by offering to draw caricatures of Allied soldiers.

This type of drawing can be considered the conceptual root of Fellini's characters, who are distinguished by their particularly expressive physique and rudimentary but outsized features. Caricature makes it possible to convey psychological traits with just a few broad strokes. Fellini, the inventor of highly arresting worlds, saw images not in purely pictorial terms but as expressions of cartoonish aggression. This approach would eventually come to fruition by unleashing a visual dream-world.

In addition to the comic strip, Fellini was always enthralled by the circus, as evident in the opening scene of *The Clowns* (1970), when a boy is awakened by a big top being put up opposite his house. Drawn by its magic, the boy goes inside, sees a wondrous world come to life in the ring and marvels at its power. This scene is especially interesting because, by using circus as the starting point, it evokes childhood as a domain under the spell of performance and comic strips, and the boy discovers a new world − the circus − endowed with a magical life force. Fellini acknowledged that this

Caricatures and cartoons

Fellini made drawings before he ever made films, producing caricatures of Hollywood actors for Rimini's Fulgor cinema at the age of seventeen and becoming one of the stars of the magazine *Marc'Aurelio* just two years later. Throughout his career, he worked out all his characters by drawing them first. In the latter years of his life he struck up a close friendship with the comic-book artist Milo Manara, who would help him turn his legendary project *Il Viaggio di G. Mastorna* into a comic strip. This background left its mark on Fellini's film work in various ways.

Firstly, there is an obvious correlation between caricature and Fellini's invented characters. The exaggeration of their physical attributes allowed him to make their outward appearances reflect their inner lives. Comic strips also provided a source of visual inspiration: when *Fellini Satyricon* (1969) came out, for example, Fellini repeatedly insisted that the film owed more to Flash Gordon than the frescos of Pompeii. Furthermore, the fragmented structure of Fellini's films reveals the strong influence of comic strips on his approach to narrative. This approach has in its turn influenced other filmmakers who take striking visual style and the construction of storyboards as their starting points: Terry Gilliam and the Caro and Jeunet duo are greatly indebted to the master, even though we may consider them deficient students.

For Fellini, drawing was not a mere preliminary to his film work, particularly using caricature in the development of his characters, but also a deep creative impulse that ran through his whole life. It is impossible to understand his work without taking into account the extensive body of graphic work, from his beginnings in *Marc'Aurelio* to his final collaboration with Manara; this ran in parallel with his adventures with film. Before it took form on the screen, Fellini's universe existed on paper, and the bold strokes of his pen largely determined the way he looked at life.

Drawing extract from *Marc'Aurelio*, published in the 1940s (How is it that the seats in the back row near the exit are cheaper than those in the front row? – It's because back there you hear the play less well.)

— Ma come?!... Le poltrone dell'ultima fila, vicino alla porta d'ingresso, costano di più di quelle delle file avanti?
— Capirete: di laggiù la commedia si sente molto meno...

scene was born from his own childhood memories and from reading *Little Nemo in Slumberland*, the comic strip created by Winsor McCay in 1905. In his book *Fare un Film* (Making a Film), Fellini described the emotions he felt sitting on his father's knee at the circus: 'When I saw the show, I was thunderstruck, as if in a flash I had recognized something that had always belonged to me and that was also my future, my work, my life.'[3]

Fellini's fascination with show business was therefore triggered by the circus and, later on, the *avanspettacolo* — variety revues that were very popular at the time. His first forays into cinema were thanks to his friendships with Ruggero Maccari and Aldo Fabrizi.[4] They both encouraged him to transpose the gags from his cartoons to variety shows, and then to the cinema. He started with *Lo vedi come sei … Lo vedi come sei?!* (1939) and *The Pirate's Dream* (1940), directed by Mario Mattoli and starring the comedian Erminio Macario. He subsequently abandoned situation comedies to write more realistic scripts, such as that of Mario Bonnard's *Peddler*

Federico Fellini in the 1940s.

and the Lady (1943), with Anna Magnani and Aldo Fabrizi, the future stars of *Rome, Open City*. The variety theatre encouraged him to break free from traditional narrative structures and adopt — from *La Dolce Vita* (1960) onwards — a model of storytelling based on a series of fragments, with no strong connecting thread. Fellini would often use theatrical revues to illustrate his love of popular entertainment. Apart from the direct homage of *Variety Lights* (1950), variety would also captivate the prostitute Cabiria in *Nights of Cabiria* (1957) and would be the ultimate expression of the illusions of the war years in *Fellini's Roma* (1972).

Rossellini and the poetry of neo-realism

In 1942 Fellini was hired to devise thrillers for the Alleanza Cinematografica Italiana (ACI), a company run by Vittorio Mussolini, the son of Benito Mussolini.[5] It was there that Fellini met the variety actress Giulietta Masina, whom he would marry a year later; in 1945 the couple had a child who died two weeks after birth. It was also at ACI that Fellini first met Roberto Rossellini, who would later ask him to persuade Aldo Fabrizi to play the part of Don Pietro in *Rome, Open City*. Fellini was then in his turn asked to collaborate on the screenplay and write some of the film's dialogue.[6] Despite the impact of *Rome, Open City* on neo-realism, it was *Paisan*, released in 1946, that really launched Fellini's career in the cinema. A film with six episodes about the liberation of Italy, *Paisan* is a journey through the ruins of the war. The fifth episode, which presents a visit to an Italian convent by three American military chaplains from different confessions, was mainly written by Fellini; he brought a Franciscan dimension to the ecumenical relationships between the trio, who come from different cultures but share the same humility. This episode anticipates the examinations of spirituality that Fellini would conduct in the 1950s.

Despite their close relationship, Rossellini and Fellini had diametrically opposed conceptions of cinema. While Fellini saw a film as something to be constructed and controlled, Rossellini was more anarchic, encouraging improvisation and sometimes even abandoning the set and leaving his assistants to shoot certain scenes. This is how Fellini found himself behind a camera for the first time, directing some shots for the fourth episode of *Paisan* in

Roberto Rossellini, Federico Fellini and Giulietta Masina during the shooting of Roberto Rossellini's *Paisan* (1946).

Top: Roberto Rossellini's *The Flowers of St. Francis* (1950).

Bottom: Roberto Rossellini's *Paisan* (1946).

Opposite page: Federico Fellini in the 1960s.

Florence. The neo-realist approach of *Paisan* was also evident in the screenplays that Fellini wrote for two renowned directors: Alberto Lattuada — with whom he shared a particularly formative experience in *Senza pietà* (1948) — and Pietro Germi, for whom he wrote, among others, *In the Name of the Law* (1949).[7]

The adventure of *Paisan* consolidated a process of mutual influence between Rossellini and Fellini. Both sought to open up a dimension that went beyond social realism, and their collaboration would deepen with 'Il miracolo' (1948), *The Flowers of St. Francis* (1950), *Europa '51* (1952) and *Dov'è la libertà …?* (1954). The first three of these films pondered the question of spirituality, albeit without ever accepting Catholic orthodoxy. Rossellini and Fellini brought faith into conflict with reality, pointing out how charity born of political awareness of social ills can lead to madness in a world dominated by unbending ideology.

The presence of a figure as magnetic as Rossellini in Fellini's early career has given rise to much speculation. Tullio Kezich, the author of a biography on Fellini, states that he 'would, on the one hand, say that Rossellini taught him everything and, on the other, that he had learnt nothing at all from Rossellini.'[8] In fact, to weigh up the artistic relationship between the two men, it is necessary to go beyond neo-realism and their relative contributions, particularly with respect to the screenplay for *Rome, Open City*. Fellini learned then from Rossellini, as Gianni Rondolino has observed, that looking at the world means going beyond appearances, 'introducing a new and original dramatic dimension and discovering the motivations hidden behind the facts'.[9] Rossellini initiated Fellini in this conception of reality, which was fundamental to the critical thinking of post-war Europe and led it to react against objective constructions of the world. In the field of cinema, André Bazin was the great theoretical champion of this approach.[10] The debate about whether reality should be constructed or whether it should be reproduced began to take into account the existence of mystery as a sign of the invisible. A human being is not merely a social creature, as he or she is also subject to existential problems. Fellini came to realize that our understanding of reality is devoid of any sense if we ignore the constitutive elements of culture, and more especially the elements involved in the construction of the personality.

Beyond neo-realism

From *Variety Lights* to *Nights of Cabiria*

Giulietta Masina in *Nights of Cabiria* (1957).

The revelation of illusion

At the end of *Variety Lights* (1950), Fellini's first film (co-directed with Alberto Lattuada), Liliana (Carla Del Poggio) abandons the provincial revue circuit to establish herself in the city and seek success in music hall. Sitting in a compartment on a train heading for Rome, she sees the actors from her company boarding another train, on their way to perform in another town. Liliana's journey takes her away from the provinces to urban cosmopolitanism, but also away from outmoded forms of entertainment to newer ones. It is as if Fellini wanted to turn over a new leaf and look to the future, albeit in the knowledge that he had to forsake an era and lifestyle that had formed part of his sentimental education. Like Fellini, Liliana thinks that she has definitively broken away from variety theatre, without realizing that variety represents her life-blood, her origins.

Variety Lights reflects the upheavals of post-war Italy but it is also a tribute to the actors who scraped a living in shabby provincial theatres. The film's rhythm and editing reveal Lattuada's classicism, but some directorial devices are clearly Felliniesque: for example, the use of the passage from night to day as a time for encounters and confessions. The film proved a commercial failure but, after the long trek through neo-realism, it highlighted the need for a certain degree of illusion. In his subsequent film, *The White Sheik* (1952), Fellini began to focus more fully on this need.

In more than one respect, *The White Sheik* can be considered a blueprint for Fellini's main obsessions, particularly the relationship between dream and reality. Here Fellini creates two thematic motifs that would soon become the twin prongs of his poetic vision: the figure of a naive simpleton who provides a visionary counterpoint to the prevailing materialism, and the quest for a place in which illusions can be constructed. *The White Sheik* also marked the start of some long-lasting collaborations: firstly with the screenwriter Tullio Pinelli, who would be responsible for all Fellini's scripts (from *I vitelloni*, 1953, onwards, in conjunction with Ennio Flaiano) until *Juliet of the Spirits* (1965); secondly, with the composer Nino Rota, whose music fitted Fellini's world perfectly.

In *The White Sheik*, Wanda, a provincial woman on honeymoon in Rome, runs away and plunges into a dream world in order to find her white sheik. Wanda is a devoted reader of photo-stories. Like a latter-day Madame Bovary, she manages to escape

15

the constraints of her world through reading, and takes love stories between Arab princes and odalisques at their face value. The particular place in which illusions can be constructed is the beach at Ostia, where a director is shooting scenes for a photo-story. Under the pine trees, a group of extras dressed in the style of *A Thousand and One Nights* brings to life a carnival world in which fiction seems to ceaselessly cross the frontier between objectivity and subjectivity. In this laboratory of fictions, Wanda creates her own reality. When her coveted white sheik appears on a swing, she follows him into a dream world, as if he had dropped from the sky, and her vision transfigures reality to penetrate the paradise of dreams.

A naive character whose gaze is laden with illusions, Wanda turns her surroundings into poetry. She weaves her way onto the set of the shoot, a world in which the backstage behind the dream is clearly visible. Wanda is, however, incapable of perceiving any artifice or anticipating that at some point this illusory world will cease to be real. The White Sheik, as played by Alberto Sordi, soon turns out to be a womanizer whose appearance betrays the most banal ordinariness. As Jacqueline Risset has observed in a perceptive essay about this film, by focusing on the theme of viewpoint, Fellini sparked off 'one of the most specific effects of his cinema: the simultaneity, or near-simultaneity, of illusion and disillusion'.[11] Furthermore, in the closing scenes

Variety Lights (1950).

of the film, the White Sheik is not merely a mirage from a photo-story — he also stands as a model for Catholic faith. Wanda's husband is obsessed with the idea of seeing the Pope, and after the couple's reconciliation they join other newly-weds in the square of the Vatican to be greeted by the pontiff. The Pope thus also appears, in his turn, as a vision, a kind of white sheik of Catholicism.

Travellers going nowhere

The White Sheik has been re-evaluated over time and is now regarded as crucial to the evolution of Fellini's poetic vision, but it attracted little attention in its day. Fellini was only really recognized as a filmmaker in 1953, when he won the Silver Lion

at the Venice Film Festival for *I vitelloni*. The story unfurls in a provincial town not unlike Rimini, Fellini's birthplace. The characters are young men from good, lower-middle-class provincial families and the locations evoke landmarks from Fellini's youth. The film closes with Moraldo leaving for Rome, just as Fellini had done at the age of nineteen. A voice-over strengthens the film's links with autobiography: an unidentified *vitellone*, haunted by his own ghosts, guides us through these images from a world with limited horizons.

Everything in *I vitelloni* seems to hark back to a key period in Fellini's youth, as if it were a kind of pseudo-autobiographical essay. Nevertheless, this kingdom of memories was reconstructed not

Dante Maggio, Carla del Poggio, Checco Durante, Peppino De Filippo and Giulietta Masina in *Variety Lights* (1950).

Following pages: Alberto Sordi and Brunella Bovo in *The White Sheik* (1952).

in Rimini but in Ostia, as if to emphasize that what is being depicted is not reality but reinvention.

The neologism *vitelloni* conveys the idea of a bunch of insipid characters, forever trapped in the planning phase without really knowing what to do with their lives. As prisoners of their own little world, incapable of moving beyond it, they are travellers going nowhere. The five main characters represent different aspects of provincial mediocrity. The central figure, Fausto (Franco Fabrizi), is a philanderer who resorts to lies and hypocrisy to cover up his affairs. He loses his job because he tries to seduce his boss's wife and ends up prey to a pathetic obsession, attempting to find a woman who left him after discovering his affair with a dancer. Alberto (Alberto Sordi) is the most ridiculous of the lot. Living off his family, he is hung up about his effeminate personality and jealously stalks his sister Olga. Leopoldo (Leopoldo Trieste) is caught up in his fantasy of being a great poet, while being supported financially by his aunts. Riccardo (Riccardo Fellini, Federico's brother) also forms part of the group but his life remains in the shadows, maybe out of inhibition on the part of the filmmaker. Finally, Moraldo (Franco Interlenghi) is a young man who observes the people around him, passing moral judgement from a distance. In order to inveigle his way into the group and provide a false biographical tone, Fellini establishes a strange split personality, divided between Moraldo and the voice of the narrator, who seems to be a sixth *vitellone* describing this reinvented world from an indeterminate vantage point.

All these characters wear masks, to deceive the world around them and to try to control it. The narrative, which largely focuses on the trials and tribulations of Fausto, is highly complex, with three intense highpoints that foreshadow Fellini's predilection for looking at the world through the prism of spectacle. The first is the election of Miss Siren, which allows Fellini to sketch in the characters of the group, and of Fausto in particular. The second is the carnival, where the spotlight falls on Alberto who, dressed as a woman, ends up dancing pathetically with his arms round a *papier mâché* head, the grotesqueness of the scene contrasting with the

Franco Fabrizi, Alberto Sordi, Leopoldo Trieste and Riccardo Fellini in *I vitelloni* (1953).

character's solitude. Finally, the arrival of a variety troupe, reminiscent of *Variety Lights*, brings into focus the aspirations of Leopoldo, obsessed with a has-been actor whom he considers a maestro. These three events allow Fellini to pinpoint the sadness of the *vitelloni*, trapped behind the walls of their own indolence. It is not just that they lie; what is worse is that they lie to themselves.

The city to which Moraldo escapes at the end of *I vitelloni* takes on a Kafkaesque hue in the short 'Agenzia matrimoniale' (1953). Here Rome is a mysterious city with sumptuous palaces that conceals the strange people who would later be examined in *La Dolce Vita* and *Fellini's Roma*. Like the two other shorts that Fellini has contributed to anthologies of

sketches, 'Agenzia matrimoniale' represents a transition that opens up unexplored territory. Here the point of departure was the omnibus film *Love in the City*, assembled by Cesare Zavattini to examine the effect of city life on amorous behaviour.[12] Zavattini was committed to documenting daily life in its most intimate dimension and matching screen time as closely as possible to real time, but Fellini distanced himself from these preoccupations. 'Agenzia matrimoniale' tells the story of a journalist who passes as a customer of a marriage agency in order to find a woman prepared to marry a werewolf. Fellini merely used Zavattini's concept as a launching pad and shot a fantasy that reflects on the strangeness that can be induced by an urban environment.

Alberto Sordi in *I vitelloni* (1953).

Anthony Quinn and Giulietta Masina in *La strada* (1954).

A world stripped of love

As the emerging economic miracle offered glimpses of a society blessed with material well-being, Italy's moral and physical horizons were gradually shifting. The basic problems were no longer those of staying afloat financially — as in the case of the unemployed worker Antonio Ricci in Vittorio De Sica's *Bicycle Thieves* (1948) — but were more existential in nature. This was a period when one part of European society believed in the absolute truths proclaimed by the dominant ideologies — Christianity and communism — while the other part turned to existentialism to understand the causes of an interior malaise. The trilogy comprising *La strada* (1954), *The Swindle* (1955) and *Nights of Cabiria* (1957) put

Fellini in the heart of the debates running through European cinema — debates sparked off by filmmakers such as Ingmar Bergman and Michelangelo Antonioni. These films delved into the way the primacy of material values has led to an inner vacuum and fomented indifference in human relationships. They ask whether redemption is possible in a world stripped of love. All three films revolve around vulnerable creatures in the throes of a moral crisis who quickly seem to represent the spectres of an errant humanity in a time of great spiritual tension. Drawing on the iconography of neo-realism to ponder the ambiguity of the real world, Fellini entered cinematic modernity, then still very much in its infancy.

Giulietta Masina in *La strada* (1954).

Right: drawing by Federico Fellini.

Following pages: Giulietta Masina and Anthony Quinn in *La strada* (1954).

La strada is the story of a journey to the sea, along a route leading from emptiness to revelation. The surroundings are the leftovers of postwar poverty, but the poetic flight of fancy that dominates the film transforms the apparent desolation. More obviously than in his previous films, Fellini here depicts the process of his characters' transformation through caricature. As André Bazin observed, 'his characters are never defined by their personality but exclusively by their appearance'.[13] Gelsomina (Giulietta Masina) is a dreamer whose innocence and simplicity undermine the cruelty of the world. Her character has the air of an archetype descended from the *commedia dell'arte*, a clownish quality that sometimes recalls Charlie Chaplin — except that Gelsomina and Chaplin's tramp do not share the same approach to action.[14] In order to act, Gelsomina does not resort to slapstick or mischief; she is above all a person who observes. Her innocence shines through her face and her vulnerability is unsettling in a world indifferent to love. Gelsomina is faced by Zampanò (Anthony Quinn), who represents the human beast, strength in its raw state, incapable of seeing beyond the material and constantly flirting with evil. The third character is the Fool (Richard Basehart), who symbolically represents air, and thus appears for the first time as a tightrope walker, moreover one equipped with wings. This airiness contrasts with the earthiness of Zampanò. The Fool is a depository of popular wisdom but is nevertheless a victim of his destiny, condemned to die tragically.

La strada examines the insensitivity and power relationships at work within a couple. Brute force is opposed by goodness and reality seems to be transfigured. This play of oppositions gives rise to a tragedy punctuated by a crime — the murder of the Fool — and then the death of Gelsomina, who dies of a broken heart. As so often with Fellini, the final scenes take place on a beach, which becomes a symbolic site for the revelation of an internal crisis. Zampanò, who has never been able to believe in love, looks to the sky in search of a solution to his despair. Fellini brings a certain ambiguity to this gesture, thereby forcing the viewer to question Zampanò's supposed redemption, or route to salvation.

La strada met with enormous popular success, crowned by an Oscar for best foreign film, but it also set off a fierce critical debate. Marxist commentators, in particular Guido Aristarco, the editor of the magazine *Cinema Nuovo*,[15] attacked its religious values and saw it as a betrayal of neo-realism. In contrast, André Bazin felt that Fellini started from a base of social realism and gradually turned to unveiling the ambiguity of the world.[16]

Richard Baseheart, Maria Zanoli, Franco Fabrizzi
and Broderick Crawford in *The Swindle* (1955).

Opposite page: Broderick Crawford
in *The Swindle* (1955).

The shock waves of this controversy coloured the reception of *The Swindle*, Fellini's most misunderstood film from the 1950s.[17] Its characters are continuations of the layabouts of *I vitelloni*. As the economic miracle had introduced a Protestant work ethic into Mediterranean culture, these good-for-nothings find themselves obliged to do something with their lives. So, they become conmen.

In the very first sequence, Fellini puts his cards on the table and reveals the mechanics of performance. Augusto (Broderick Crawford) disguises himself as a bishop, Picasso (Richard Basehart) as a priest. Peasants are hoodwinked by these disguises, while the ancestral weight of religion, and most

particularly its rituals, provides a fertile breeding ground for false truths. The film's action takes place over the course of five days, or rather five nights and their subsequent early hours. Gradually, and paradoxically, the amused depiction of this trickery gives way to a reflection on its mechanisms. On the one hand, *The Swindle* seems to be a drama about the deceit reigning in the modern world but, on the other hand, the film can also be seen as an examination of the nature of an existential crisis, and of fear of the future.

For the first time, Fellini explored old age and its anxieties. Augusto is middle-aged and when he discovers that his daughter has left him and realizes that he cannot make amends for his past errors, he finds himself caught in a tangle of lies — the same lies that prevent him from taking action and fill him with disgust. Like Zampanò in *La strada*, Augusto is a victim of the pain he has inflicted on other people and comes to a tragic end, abandoned, dying on desolate ground, his arms outstretched in a vain search for a road to redemption. Augusto's starkly filmed Calvary is that of a man crying out in a desert. Overwhelmed by the dramatic power of this scene, François Truffaut wrote in his account of the Venice Film Festival: 'I would willingly spend hours watching Broderick Crawford die.'[18]

Fellini at work: 'Journal of *The Swindle*'

Dominique Delouche worked as assistant director on The Swindle, Nights of Cabiria *and* La Dolce Vita. *His experiences alongside Fellini were recorded in Cahiers du cinéma as 'Journal de Il bidone' (Journal of* The Swindle*). This document provides an invaluable resource for understanding Fellini's working methods, particularly during the shooting of the New Year's Eve party in the Titanus Studio, Rome, 10–17 June 1955.*

We shall shoot chronologically, which is not the most economic solution (as it is necessary to retain all the extras and actors for the whole period) but it is one that helps the director develop his inspiration.

The choice of faces and the deliberate blurring between man and beast recall Hieronymus Bosch. [...] Fellini gives his personal attention to each and every one of his extras, whom he addresses familiarly, by name. He creates a friendly atmosphere while also being very demanding.

It seems to me that in this setting Fellini works on three levels: the psychological, the atmospheric and the metaphysical. The first manifests itself in close-ups, in the faces – especially that of Rinaldo, a genuine conman, his gaze steeped in cocaine, his chin weak, his baldness disguised. He makes one think of the debauched characters in Pavese's novels. As for atmosphere, that's in the frenzied whoring, the unbridled pleasure, the cigarette smoke, the abundant flesh, the foaming champagne. The metaphysics lie in the Dantesque vision, the picture of lust.

Good will at work, which sometimes also means patience, is at heart a sign of a director's supremacy. Disorder and disrespect on his set never ruffle him, as he is always sure that he is the boss and that he can command obedience whenever he wants. When somebody's personal initiative derails his plans, instead of rejecting it and sticking to his guns, he very often turns it round and appropriates it. So many directors turn on their crew if it comes up with ideas, to convince themselves that they are in control, to dispel any uncertainties, difficulties and nerves. Anybody arriving on set at that moment would think they had entered an aquatic dream. The camera movement is particularly delicate and Fellini, his eye at the view-finder, has demanded the most absolute silence. The lamps resemble the headlight of a submarine. Couples dance on the spot so as not to lose their marks, swaying like seaweed. Three women are sprawled on an armchair: an oyster with a pearl, a coral reef and a sawfish. Some shellfish are on the carpet. The boom operator and Martelli pointing his hand-held lamp at the faces seem like two deep-sea divers. All this is wonderfully absurd in the silence and half-light, taking one back to being an innocent spectator and making one forget the whys and wherefores of cinema.

This is an extract from Dominique Delouche, 'Journal de *Il bidone*', *Cahiers du cinéma*, 57 (March 1956).

Richard Baseheart and Broderick Crawford in *The Swindle* (1955).

Opposite page: Federico Fellini on the set of *The Swindle* (1955).

Nights of Cabiria is the story of a woman who wants to be loved. Cabiria (Giulietta Masina) is another dreamer, but unlike Gelsomina, she is not defenceless. She is a prostitute with no sense of guilt and considers herself to be living a normal life. In one key scene she watches a magician in a variety theatre, responds to his request for a volunteer to come to the stage and ends up being hypnotized. She then tells the audience of her desire for a new life, of her dreams of getting married, having children and a house. When she wakes up, none of her wishes has come true — they are crushed by the force of reality. Yet again, this scene manifests the dialectic — already expounded in *The White Sheik* — between the world of performance as the source of illusions and the more inhospitable real world.

Cabiria's desires have nothing in common with those of the bourgeois morality that are the staple of traditional melodrama. Cabiria wants to love in a world that has been deprived of love, but does not call into question her work — prostitution — or look for an easier life. She is content to remain hopeful, while her existence is full of wretchedness and disillusion. In one early scene — one that echoes Hollywood's depictions of romantic love — she is about to be embraced by an occasional lover but is astonished to find herself being robbed and pushed into the river. She undergoes a similar humiliation in a later scene.

The film's fragmented structure allows Fellini to show a number of settings without any causal logic. Characters wander through places that end up becoming worlds of their own. A tension is established between the deliberately over-the-top set pieces — the procession to the Sanctuary of the Virgin, the party in the nightclub — and the moments of solitude in which Cabiria ponders on bringing her dreams to life. The narrative thus starts to break free from the tyranny of plot, allowing each scene to take on a greater autonomy and prefiguring the episodic structure of *La Dolce Vita*. *Nights of Cabiria* also prompted a cooler attitude towards Fellini from Catholics, who had looked favourably on his early work but were now dismayed by the film's focus on prostitution.

François Périer and Giulietta Masina in *Nights of Cabiria* (1957).

Following pages: Giulietta Masina and Amadeo Nazzari in *Nights of Cabiria* (1957).

After the economic miracle

From *La Dolce Vita* to *Amarcord*

Marcello Mastroianni and Anita Ekberg
in *La Dolce Vita* (1960).

Following pages: Marcello Mastroianni
in *La Dolce Vita* (1960).

The new Babylon

By the end of the 1950s Fellini had become extremely popular, largely thanks to his second Oscar (for *Nights of Cabiria*), and he now enjoyed great freedom. He was going through a personal crisis, however, on account of the death of his father, Urbano. At that time the bourgeois lifestyle exhibited with such enthusiasm in Rome was acquiring a magnetic attraction. Having been blessed with a life of ease by the economic miracle, Italians started to take advantage of ephemeral pleasures, while the media gradually created the conditions for a new society of spectacle. These were the years in which Rome became a haven for decadent American stars who dreamed of building a Hollywood *sul Tevere* (Hollywood-on-Tiber), a paradise where the strains of jazz in cabarets set the tone for the night life, and where the beautiful people of the Caffè Society were pursued by paparazzi in search of a scoop at any price. As a participant in this *dolce vita*, this sweet life, Fellini recorded the spirit of the age in the Cinecittà studios in an attempt to fathom the decadence of a western civilization that had turned Rome into the new Babylon.

La Dolce Vita presents a series of characters who dive headlong into pleasure in search of some degree of happiness. Marcello Rubini (Marcello Mastroianni) is both a witness to and participant in this ferment, a man without qualities caught between his frustrated intellectual aspirations and his desire to gain access to the city's hotspots — and the zombies who frequent them. Fellini is Marcello and he observes him with complicity, free from any condemnatory moral posturing.

The film is built around four parties reminiscent of debauched bacchanals. The first celebrates the arrival of a movie star, Sylvia (Anita Ekberg). The second involves a group of intellectuals — gravitating around the writer Steiner (Alain Cuny) — who refuse to live in a world they consider predictable. The guests at the third party are corrupt aristocrats, ghosts from another age performing their rituals in the ruins of the past. Finally, the last party features brainless artists, assembled almost at random to make an exhibition of themselves in humiliating circumstances. A dream-like heaviness hangs over every scene, which invariably ends with a painful return to reality, as if every pleasurable situation inevitably has to end in post-coital sadness. So, after making love with the well-heeled Maddalena in a prostitute's bed, Marcello has to come to the rescue of his fiancée, who has

tried to kill herself. Similarly, after spending a night at a seance with the aristocrats, he discovers that Steiner has murdered his children and then committed suicide. In the final scene, at dawn, a group of bourgeois, having played at striptease, discover a sinister, bloated fish on a beach. Marcello then sees a girl but he cannot communicate with her, perhaps because nobody entering this new Babylon is able to recapture any past innocence.

The rhythm of the parties is punctuated by the omnipresence of the paparazzi. Whereas in *I vitelloni* and *The Swindle* lying was a theatrical game with masks, in the new society of the spectacle, reality is created by the flashes of news photographers. They have acquired the power to create a false religious miracle and they ravage intimacy,

even of the most painful kind. This is the case, for example, when Steiner's wife, still unaware of her family's tragedy, is hounded by photographers and poses in front of them like an actress.

In the year when Michelangelo Antonioni stunned audiences with *L'avventura* (1960),[19] Fellini hurtled into modernity with *La Dolce Vita*. His films would no longer aim at an objective representation of a coherent world but would instead be compulsive unveilings of an ephemeral universe, devoid of any sense. Fellini conceived *La Dolce Vita* as an open work, structured around a series of dreadful places peopled by actors with faces that are generally caricaturesque. After this film, Fellini's stories would gradually become 'climaxes, curves of dramatic temporality. In fact, every sequence is a turn.'[20]

La Dolce Vita (1960).

Marcello Mastroianni and Anita Ekberg in *La Dolce Vita* (1960).

Male/female

Unsettled by the success of *La Dolce Vita* and the scandal it provoked in some conservative quarters, Fellini went into psychoanalysis. Dr Ernst Bernhard introduced him to the theories of Carl Gustav Jung and made him understand that, contrary to the Freudian notion that symbols in dreams are merely a translation of repression, the unconscious can also be a repository for a richly poetic imaginary world. Reading Jung enabled Fellini to explore the symbolism of the collective unconscious and convinced him that irrational images can be emotionally captivating. Fellini himself acknowledged that it was Jung who allowed him to make his cinema 'a meeting point between science and magic, between rationality and imagination.'[21] He started to envisage a cinema with no borders between the real and the imaginary, a cinema immersed in the psyche. The influence of Jungian psychiatry led Fellini to analyse his own male ego in *8½* (1963) and reflect on femininity as a complex otherness in *Juliet of the Spirits* (1965). Fiction gave rise to a series of mirror images, with characters serving as phantasmagorical doubles for Fellini or Giulietta Masina.

Fellini's first evident use of dream structures occurred in 1962, in the mid-length feature 'The Temptation of Dr. Antonio', part of the anthology film *Boccaccio '70*.[22] The basic story is that of a man inhibited by moral conventions who feels an enormous sexual attraction for the image of Anita Ekberg on a huge billboard advertising milk. Fellini delves into the confrontation between morality and sexual desire, while reflecting on images as stimuli for collective desires.

Fellini and women

Fellini explores the way in which the new society of material comforts has plunged traditional machismo into a crisis and opened up the way for a newly independent woman. For Fellini, women represent above all the mystery of otherness. His female universe is protean but, although it exhibits many different types, some of them are mere caricatures that exist only in the male imagination.

The first female figure to emerge in Fellini's films was that of the ingenuous dreamer, portrayed above all by Giulietta Masina. In *The White Sheik* this dreamer is Wanda (Brunella Bovo), who constantly transforms the reality around her into poetry. Gelsomina in *La strada*, Cabiria in *Nights of Cabiria* and Amelia in *Ginger and Fred* are other naive women whose reveries provide a substitute for harsh everyday existence. Giulietta (Juliet) in *Juliet of the Spirits* embodies the prototype of the unhappy housewife whose suffering does not spare her husband, riven by his own contradictions and confronted, through her, by his own feelings of guilt. Like Nora in *Ibsen's Doll's House*, she decides to escape from her husband's clutches. This housewife figure seems unstable and full of contradictions. As for the lover/fiancée, she is exemplified by Emma (Yvonne Furneaux) in *La Dolce Vita*, whose sole aspiration is to possess her fiancé. When a woman becomes an independent spouse, like Luisa (Anouk Aimée) in *8½*, she shows less mercy as she is less inclined to believe her husband's excuses. Women also expose male excesses, as in *City of Women*, where Snàporaz's wife (Alessandra Panelli) accuses him of being an egoist obsessed with women as sex objects.

The figure of the wife is contrasted with that of the sensual mistress, often flaunting the physique of an old-time Hollywood star. She is matchlessly incarnated by Sandra Milo in *8½* and *Juliet of the Spirits*, and by Magali Noël as Gradisca in *Amarcord*. This type of woman, lusted after by teenagers, can go on to become the submissive mistress of adult men.

Another Felliniesque type is the woman with hypertrophied sexual attributes, representing pure animal libido: the buxom tobacconist (Maria Antonietta Beluzzi) in *Amarcord*, La Saraghina, who initiates teenagers on the beach in *8½*, the prostitutes in the brothels of *Fellini's Roma*. All these women prefigure the grotesque and decadent sexuality that permeates the imaginary worlds of *Fellini's Casanova* and *City of Women*.

Fellini also explores the image of the unattainable ideal woman – the legendary movie star, such as Anita Ekberg in *La Dolce Vita*, the untouchable virgin, such as Claudia (Claudia Cardinale) in *8½*. If the ideal woman is ever conquered, she turns into an automaton: this is the case with the mechanical doll who is Casanova's final dance partner.

Anouk Aimée in *8½* (1963).
Bottom, left: Claudia Cardinale in *8½* (1963).
Bottom, right: Marcello Mastroianni and Yvonne Furneaux in *La Dolce Vita* (1960).

Opposite page:
Top: Federico Fellini and Giulietta Masina on the set of *Nights of Cabiria* (1957).
Bottom: Anita Ekberg in *La Dolce Vita* (1960).

Edra Gale (right) in *8½* (1963).

Opposite page: Marcello Mastroianni on the set of *8½* (1963).

Following pages: Marcello Mastroianni and Sandra Milo in *8½* (1963).

The unruly oneirism of 'The Temptation of Dr. Antonio' is continued in the dreamlike dimension apparent in the opening images of 8½. Guido Anselmi (Marcello Mastroianni) is stuck in a suffocating traffic jam. He gets out of his car and flies onwards like a kite, above the cars, and then floats above a beach. Attached to a cord, he is manoeuvred by his lawyer. This scene points the way for a film that concentrates on the inner life of the artist. Guido wants to create on the basis of his sensations and dreams. He breaks free in the beginning and starts to soar on flights of imagination before being recaptured by reality and its many voices. After this start, 8½ is conceived as a complex system of superimposed layers in which the contents of the story are inseparable from its mode of construction.

It is a reflection not only on cinema but also on the experience of a director in permanent conflict with his own imagination, a director who makes his own angst the subject of his work. The confusion intrinsic to existence is therefore the impetus for the unusual creative process that gave rise to 8½, the mouthpiece for a new cinema that separated narrative from viewpoint.[23]

Guido Anselmi is a mirror image of Fellini, a narcissist determined to put his entire universe into his work but reluctant to opt for one specific creative approach. Using a fictional character, Fellini struggles with his own insecurity at a time when he seems to have reached the summit but feels that he is in conflict with his conscience. He gives form to his demons, reappropriates the frustrations of his childhood and

Sandra Milo and Marcello Mastroianni in *8½* (1963).

Opposite page: Marcello Mastroianni in *8½* (1963).

chooses dreams as the way to fulfil his unsatisfied desires, while searching for harmony in the chaos of the real. Although the film is nominally about the shooting of a science-fiction fable, the overriding feeling is that the work that Guido Anselmi is in the process of creating is none other than *8½* itself. The attacks and accusations hurled at the unmade film allow Fellini to exorcise his own fears and steel himself against possible criticisms. The fear of continuing to go forwards leads to a simulated suicide in the closing scenes, before the director is reborn, with all the characters in his universe parading in a great celebration of creativity and vitality.

The meta-narrative of *8½* also summons up the various female figures that would recur throughout Fellini's subsequent films. Firstly, there is the opposition between Carla (Sandra Milo), the ideal mothering mistress, and Luisa (Anouk Aimée), the wife whose love life is complicated by being beside a man who fantasizes about other types of women. The other key woman is Claudia (Claudia Cardinale), the perfect but inaccessible woman of semi-divine beauty. Gloria (Barbara Steele) is a pedantic pseudo-intellectual who cannot see beyond the world of appearances. Finally, La Saraghina is a grotesque figure who harks back to teenage sexual impulses. Guido brings all his women

The *auteur* and his doubles

Much of Fellini's work deals with the elaboration of an invented autobiography, allowing the imagination to broaden life's horizons. Fellini does not express himself in the first person singular, however; instead, he uses a series of doubles that reflect some of his many facets. Childhood comes to the surface when the young Fellini discovers the circus in *The Clowns*. In *Fellini's Roma* the same child is at school, rambling on about the myths of ancient Rome. *Amarcord* is entirely devoted to adolescence, but instead of adopting one specific double, Fellini projected his memories onto various characters, giving pride of place to his old school chum Titta. *I vitelloni* is obviously set in the world of Fellini's youth, and it

is equally obvious that Moraldo (Franco Interlenghi) – who like him escapes to Rome in 1939 – resembles him in some respects. Fellini borrowed some ideas from a screenplay that was never filmed, *Moraldo in Città*, for the character of the young provincial (Peter Gonzales) in *Fellini's Roma* who discovers his sexuality in the city's brothels. The identification is not total but, despite the differences, there is clearly something of Fellini in this young man driven by the desire to enjoy the city's hidden pleasures. The idealized image of these early years in Rome recurs in *Fellini's Intervista*, in the character of the young journalist (Sergio Rubini) longing to interview a star from Cinecittà. Marcello Mastroianni, present

in six of Fellini's full-length features, is his double *par excellence*. In *La Dolce Vita*, their first collaboration, Mastroianni played Marcello, the journalist shambling through the artificial nirvanas of Rome's moneyed classes. Marcello provides the narrative thread and, like Fellini, chronicles a lifestyle that is also his own. In *8½* the process of identification is more complex. Fellini and Anselmi are filmmakers in the creative doldrums who project their fantasies onto the world around them. Fellini uses Mastroianni to manifest his inner soul. He makes a brief appearance in *Fellini: A Director's Notebook*, while in *City of Women* Guido Anselmi has become Snàporaz. Here the double is plunged into

the phantasmagoric world of the female unconscious, lost in dreams and nightmares springing from desire. There is a wealth of virtual doubles in *Ginger and Fred*. Here Mastroianni is Pippo, who, like Fellini, is alienated by the falseness of the new world around him. Fellini–Mastroianni recovers his female *alter ego* Amelia (Giulietta Masina) but they both feel powerless when confronted with the passing of time.

In *Fellini's Intervista* Fellini's play with his double is rather more sophisticated. He is seen making up his young *alter ego* (Sergio Rubini) but later comes across Marcello transformed into Mandrake the Magician and accompanies him into the mists of the past.

Giulietta Masina and Sandra Milo in *Juliet of the Spirits* (1965).

together in a domestic harem and tries to dominate them, considering them part of his own psyche.

From 8½ onwards, Fellini's cinema acquired a therapeutic component. The characters are more and more caricatured, the boundaries between fiction and reality are increasingly blurred and there is frequent recourse to showing films within films — all these factors contribute to the complex depiction of Fellini's inner world. *Juliet of the Spirits* is the opposite of 8½. Here the subject under analysis is a woman, played by Fellini's wife, Giulietta Masina. The whole film is haunted by spirits, symbolic incarnations of the repressive demons of a woman stifled by the constraints of married life. Marital break-up is the main theme of the narrative, which follows the emancipation of Giulietta. Her husband, Giorgio (Mario Pisu), is reminiscent of Guido Anselmi and seems a caricature of Fellini based on certain archetypal features. The wife attains liberation by gaining awareness of her own condition as a woman and returning to herself.

This inner journey is presented as an exorcism, punctuated by a series of incursions into the domain of childhood (Giulietta playing a martyred saint) and family mythology (the story of the grandfather who ran off with a circus dancer). Giulietta is ceaselessly comparing her own image as a demure housewife with that of other women. Sexuality is represented by the character of the neighbour, Susy (Sandra Milo, in a role similar to that she had in 8½), while the over-protective and excessively devoted mother checks Giulietta's childhood impulses.

From the very first sequence, Giulietta seems lost in her surroundings, as if she is living in a doll's house. Her life depends entirely on her husband and when she suspects him of being unfaithful she searches for the truth in spiritualism and hires a private detective. Her liberation requires more than coming to terms with the figure of the husband, however; she also has to find herself by throwing off the psychic shackles of old mythologies. Shot in colour, *Juliet of the Spirits* plays in a particularly interesting way with three symbolic colours: the red, white and green of the Italian flag.

Opposite page: Sandra Milo and Giulietta Masina in *Juliet of the Spirits* (1965).

Sandra Milo, Giulietta Masina and Valentina Cortese in *Juliet of the Spirits* (1965).

Terence Stamp in 'Toby Dammit' (1968).

The threshold of death

In 1965 Fellini was unhappy at the lukewarm reception given to *Juliet of the Spirits*. For the first time in his career, no festival was interested in the film so it went straight into the cinemas. The critics were unenthusiastic, dismissing the work as chaotic and self-indulgent, while the Italian Centro Cattolico Cinematografico (Catholic Cinematographic Center) advised the faithful to stay away. Fellini was going through a serious professional crisis: the screenwriters Ennio Flaiano and Tullio Pinelli ended a collaboration of fifteen years and Gianni Di Venanzo, the cameraman on his most recent films, died of hepatitis. Fellini felt lonely and abandoned by his friends, apart from the loyal Nino Rota. To overcome this bad patch, he started to write, in conjunction with Dino Buzzati, the screenplay for *Il Viaggio di G. Mastorna*, the story of an aeroplane caught in a fierce snowstorm that has to make an emergency landing in an unknown city. Among the passengers is Mastorna, who realizes, after wandering in a strange world, that he has crossed the threshold of death. The project was beset by numerous mishaps. The Dino De Laurentiis production company raised the necessary finance and elaborate sets were built, but then Fellini suffered a heart attack that put him in hospital and very nearly killed him. During his long period of convalescence, he wrote *La mia Rimini*,[24] after which personal problems forced him to give up the *Mastorna* project. The idea would never leave him, however — to such an extent that it became the main source of inspiration for his later films. *Mastorna* marked the beginning of a darker, more pessimistic phase.

The first evidence of this new period would be 'Toby Dammit' (1968), a mid-length feature that formed part of the Franco—Italian production *Spirits of the Dead*.[25] It was based on a story by Edgar Allan Poe, although its real starting point was the image of a half-destroyed bridge and a head severed by barbed wire. The film shows the steps that lead a man to this cruel and fateful end. 'Toby Dammit' starts with a turbulent plane journey to Rome (echoes of *Mastorna*). The camera then follows an egocentric, alcoholic actor (Terence Stamp) as he hobnobs with the rich and famous. He is in Italy to film a kind of 'Catholic western'. After an awards ceremony, he hurtles off at the wheel of a red Ferrari through a hallucinatory landscape lit solely by the car's headlights. Finally, he meets his death, decapitated on a

Fellini Satyricon (1969).

ruined bridge shrouded in fog, while a young she-devil observes the scene. 'Toby Dammit' lays bare a reality from beyond the grave, as if Fellini wanted to use fiction to give form to the monsters that surged forth from his illness. It is a sombre manifesto on the difficulty of portraying death, especially when it is not an end but a starting point.

Fellini's fears and failures as a creator also come to the surface in *Fellini: A Director's Notebook* (1968). This time it is not a self-referential fiction like *8½* but rather a documentary in the form of notes towards a possible essay on Fellini's creative processes. Fellini took advantage of a commission from American television[26] to bury *Mastorna*, and so the setting is a space in ruins, symbolizing the abandonment of the project. In this film Fellini also established the broad outlines of his next feature, *Fellini Satyricon* (1969). The originality of *Fellini: A Director's Notebook* lies not in its construction but in the way in which Fellini's notes anticipate the strategy he would bring to fruition in *The Clowns* (1970), *Fellini's Roma* (1972), *Orchestra Rehearsal* (1978) and *Fellini's Intervista* (1987). All these films, seemingly created in a minor register, depart from the

'documentary' format. They have nothing to say about the empirical world but are rather fascinating writing workshops. Fellini brought to them a meta-discursive element, turning them into simulated sketches of his creative process.

In *Fellini: A Director's Notebook* Fellini evokes epic movies about ancient Rome as part of the baggage acquired by his unconscious during childhood. In *Fellini Satyricon*, however, his reinterpretation of the antiquity of Petronius is the antithesis of these old films. It is an 'anti-epic' that dissolves their colossal dimension by reconstructing the Roman age on the basis of its ruins. This lost civilization is brought back to life via atrophied images, by vestiges of the past. The murals of Pompeii triggered a larger-than-life creative approach involving dream-like settings, grotesque faces — way beyond caricature — and vivid colours. *Fellini Satyricon* is a morbid film, both bizarre and visionary.

Fellini was particularly attracted by the unfinished, fragmentary nature of Petronius' text, which allowed him to break once again with causal logic and concoct a narrative revolving around the elaboration of forms, the creation of a world. The 57

Mario Romagnoli (right),
Capucine and Magali Noël
in *Fellini Satyricon* (1969).

Rome he conceived does not seek to be a real Rome, in any historic sense, or a mythical Rome along the lines of the old epic films; it is a ghostly Rome, the capital of a civilization in crisis, devouring itself from within.

The plot is very thin. Young Encolpio is annoyed by his lover Gitone's departure with his friend Ascilto. Encolpio's loss, his search for his lover and subsequent encounter with his rival are the only pegs on which Fellini hangs a journey through this ancient world, brought up to date via an archaeological dig into the western unconscious. Encolpio's search is punctuated by visits to places haunted by death. The rich Trimalcione ends his sumptuous banquet by simulating his own death, the merchant Lica dies decapitated by invaders announcing the coming of another age, and a pair of noble patricians commit suicide. Finally, in the closing scenes, Ascilto is murdered and the poet Eumolpo dies, bequeathing his legacy to all those willing to eat his flesh. *Fellini Satyricon* examines a world in crisis, and as such it is a kind of prolongation of *La Dolce Vita* — with two main differences: in *Fellini Satyricon*, the dream-like atmosphere is more pervasive, and the sexual content — represented by orgies and a constant wavering between hetero- and homosexuality — is far more explicit.

Clowns and the city

With *Fellini Satyricon*, Fellini regained his status as an *auteur*, as well as assembling a new team, including the cameraman Giuseppe Rotunno, the screenwriter Bernardino Zapponi and the producer Alberto Grimaldi, with whom he would also make the controversial *Fellini's Casanova* (1976). The key figure among his new collaborators, however, was Danilo Donati, responsible for the sets and costumes. Donati used Fellini's drawings and caricatures as the entrance into his dream world. Production design was acquiring a crucial importance in Fellini's work, as from then on reflections on the myriad dimensions of reality gave way to an Expressionist look that endorsed the notion of cinema as a kind of demiurgic construction.[27] The Cinecittà studios, where Fellini had reconstructed the Via Veneto for *La Dolce Vita*, now became a living space as much as a workspace;

Federico Fellini on the set of *The Clowns* (1970).

Fellini's Roma (1972).

in Studio 5 he could remake the world. Here he could turn the ancient Rome of *Fellini Satyricon* and the modern city of *Fellini's Roma* into reality, just as he would with his birthplace, Rimini, in *Amarcord* (1973) and with the spooky Venice of *Fellini's Casanova*. Fellini barely left these studios even when between shoots, as he was forever looking for new actors, reading scripts or sketching new worlds. Henceforth, Fellini the modern filmmaker relentlessly investigating his own creative process would go hand in hand with a Fellini who spurned classical narrative and conjured up extravagant visions as projections of his own deliriums. *The Clowns* and *Fellini's Roma* were declarations of intent in this respect.

In *The Clowns*, Fellini states at one point that the clowns struggling away in big tops also belong to the great family of strange, monstrous creatures parading their madness in Italian provincial towns. Where do the whiteface and auguste clown-types come from? This is an important question because it highlights Fellini's caricaturesque approach to cinema. Faces exteriorize the neuroses of the soul while the grotesque contortions of clowns and madmen reveal an insanity that, like the circus, comes very close to imagination in its pure state. The auguste clown (typically, wearing multicoloured make-up and playing the role of the anarchist) reminds us that the spectacle of circus is a metaphor for the world. The whiteface clown is an Apollonian figure, the auguste clown Dionysian. *The Clowns*, produced by RAI as part of a policy to bring art cinema into public television, was conceived as a documentary tribute and featured interviews with legendary clowns. The documentary footage is complemented, however, by a depiction of the young Fellini's revelatory introduction to the circus and his sombre reflections on the demise of clowning, culminating in a circus number featuring a clown's burial — as if he, Fellini, saw the film as a requiem for the inevitable death of illusions.

Fellini's Roma (1972).

Fellini's Roma is neither a symphony celebrating a city nor a documentary about some of its more hidden places, nor even an invocation of personal experiences recaptured by visits to various locations. Even though the film does sometimes draw on all these approaches, Fellini transcends them to fashion a kaleidoscope in which the myth of the Eternal City is superimposed on reality, just as life is superimposed on dream. The seed for *Fellini's Roma* was planted by the unrealized project *Moraldo in Città*, which also fed into the preparation of *La Dolce Vita*. The majority of the film's scenes — including the arrival into the city on the motorway — were created in Studio 5 in Cinecittà.

Fellini's Roma offers an elaborate discourse involving three levels of representation. First of all, there is the city as myth. Before Rome itself even appears on the screen, we see its name on a signpost by a river, where it attracts the attention of schoolchildren from Rimini. The capital city pre-exists as the site of heroic conquests from the past, but also

as a catalyst for the desire to escape provincial life. It is a place invented in the land of children, and as such operates as an illusion.

For all that, Rome also appears as a city with a physical presence, in perpetual transformation, with its own special worlds, and with ruins and frescos lying beneath the manifestations of modern civilization. Fellini explores not only the nostalgic city that welcomed him as a young man but also the contemporary city, where he is feverishly creating. The Rome of the 1940s, with its leisurely, convivial meals on the terraces of the Trastevere and seedy revue acts, is contrasted with the Rome of the 1970s, in which Fellini appears as himself. Modern Rome is traffic jams and hippies levitating on the Spanish Steps, but it is also archaeological excavations that bring back to life paintings from the past, although they expire once again as soon as they come into contact with a present in which they do not belong.

Alongside this Rome imbued with nostalgia and the crisis of civilization, there is a third city, one

Fellini's Roma (1972).

that emerges from the projection of the unconscious, where invisible hinterlands assume such oversized proportions that they turn into veritable nightmares. In the heart of this hidden Rome, the brothels of the post-war period and those of the present provide a curious combination of the grotesque and the pathetic. This clandestine city is also the haunt of the 'black aristocracy' — closely involved in the Vatican's financial and political interests — which transforms the power of the Church into a fashion show staged as dream-like exhibitionism.[28] The epilogue is distinguished by the appearance of a woman who also symbolizes Rome — Anna Magnani, who lives on as part of another myth created by the cinema: the neo-realist film *Rome, Open City*.

Adolescence reinvented

Freudian psychoanalysis considers that experiences from the past remain in the unconscious, albeit in a disordered state. While the conscious mind organizes the transitory flux of present experience, elements from the past emerge involuntarily as projections of the psyche. In *Amarcord*[29] Fellini undertook a curious process of reinventing brief sensations from his adolescence. Memory as projection is the film's starting point, but remembering means not merely reliving but also inventing. Fellini collaborated on this project with the poet and writer Tonino Guerra, born in the same year as him, in a village just ten kilometres from Rimini. Guerra was already a renowned screenwriter, thanks to his work in the 1960s with Antonioni, Francesco Rosi and the Taviani brothers.

There is not a single shot of the real Rimini in *Amarcord*; instead the film displays a series of sets built in Studio 5 in Cinecittà, sometimes with obvious touches of fantasy, such as the plastic sea on which the inhabitants of the city sail out in search of the SS *Rex*, an ocean liner from the Fascist fleet that serves as a symbol for illusion.

Even though *Amarcord* operates as an exercise in personal remembrance, there are several narrative voices that eclipse that of Fellini. These voices expound key ideas about the family, about society, power, illusions and myths, providing a poetic compendium of Fascist provincial life. Fellini looks back at the world of his childhood with irony and nostalgia, without succumbing to sentimentality. This collective narrative has a circular form — passing through the seasons, from one spring to another — and one of its many characters — the young Titta — is more important than the rest.

La mia Rimini, by Federico Fellini

In 1967, after a brush with death following a heart attack and while still in hospital, Fellini started to write about his childhood in Rimini. This text anticipated some sequences and motifs in Amarcord, *as well as being a meditation on how to transcribe memory.*

One thing is certain: I never come to Rimini willingly. I say that with all sincerity. It is like a block. I still have family there: my mother, my sister. Fear of my own feelings? It is more the impression that every return is yet another masochistic, satisfied filtering of my memories: a spectacularly literary operation. Obviously, that has its charm. A sleepy charm. And problems. The fact that I can't manage to consider Rimini with any objectivity. It's only a dimension of my memory. Moreover, every time I'm in Rimini I'm scolded by ghosts that I thought had been banished for good.

How to talk about Rimini? A word made up of little sticks, of little soldiers in a row. I can't manage to be objective. Rimini is an indecipherable scrawl, scary and tender, with, what's more, the deep breathing of the sea, that big, open empty space. Nostalgia is better defined there, especially in winter: the Adriatic, the white crests of the waves, the strong wind.

At that time the grown-ups held court on the main street, in the café where friends met: Raoul's. It was the place to be. The owner, a very lively, tubby little man had made it, along the lines of the cafés in Milan at that time, a rendez-vous for artists, tortured youths and sporty types. There were also a few mild references to politics, but nothing more. It was here that the *vitelloni* of Rimini met in winter. The Grand Hotel, in contrast, was a fairytale abounding in opulence, luxury and oriental splendour. Whenever a description in the novels that I then used to read failed to stimulate my imagination, the Grand Hotel became my reference for the scenes that I invented. It was my backcloth, just as in some enterprising little theatres the same scenery is adapted to every situation. Crimes, kidnappings, mad nights of love, blackmail, suicide, the Torture Garden and the Goddess Kali: the Grand Hotel was the place for all types of intrigue.

From the Café Commercio, one could also see Gradisca. Sparkling like flint, in black satin clothes. We would run to press our noses against the window. When she went out, Gradisca was always dressed as if she had to go on stage, even in the depths of winter: false eyelashes (accessories that we had still barely seen), kiss-curls everywhere, an impeccable perm … When Gradisca passed in front of the café, she induced boundless appetites, enormous hunger, a crazy yearning for fresh milk.

This is an extract from Federico Fellini, *La mia Rimini*, Guaraldi, Rimini, 2003.

Titta is not Fellini's *alter ego*, however; he is in fact an evocation of his classmate, Luigi Benzi, who had already appeared in one of Fellini's comic strips in *Marc'Aurelio*. Titta is the son of a father with anarchist leanings whom the Fascists torture by forcing him to drink castor oil. He has a possessive mother, a Fascist uncle, Patacca, a grandfather who dreams of stroking the buttocks of the maids, and another uncle, Teo, who is confined to a psychiatric hospital and on one excursion climbs a tree to proclaim that he wants a woman.

Titta and his friends form a group of nascent *vitelloni* who hang around on the streets, participate in the town's festive events, bask in the lights and shadows of the Fulgor cinema and dream of make-believe paradises by spying on the people in the Grand Hotel. Women occupy a special place in this world. The beautiful Gradisca (Magali Noël) is the model of a sensual woman, as previously incarnated by Sandra Milo in *8½*. All the teenagers dream of seducing her, although the fervour of adolescent desire is more effectively satisfied by the ample breasts of the tobacconist.

The characters in *Amarcord* are drawn in broad strokes, like veritable walking caricatures. Fellini incorporates techniques from *fumetti*, popular comic strips, not only in his conception of the characters but also in his staging and storytelling. The colours used for the sets and costumes are very vivid, echoing the primary colours of the *fumetti*, while the film's open structure recalls their division of narrative into short comic scenes. Here, these scenes focus on special collective events, such as the bonfire to mark the coming of spring, the Thousand Mile car race, the arrival of the SS *Rex* and the ceremony organized in honour of a top Fascist dignitary. These scenes are interspersed with anecdotes revolving around Titta's circle of friends and Gradisca, whose marriage to an officer from the Carabinieri closes the film. The motley kaleidoscope of *Amarcord* took Fellini to new heights, where he managed to precisely balance the various elements of his style. The film also won him another Oscar for best foreign film, and it attracted those cinema-goers who had previously been put off by arthouse offerings such as *La Dolce Vita* and *8½*. Fellini would never know this kind of success again.

Amarcord (1973).

Confronting the neo-television empire

From *Fellini's Casanova* to *La voce della luna*

Federico Fellini in *Fellini's Intervista* (1987).

From Fellini to Felliniesque

In his colossal biography, Tullio Kezich tells how Fellini, dejected by the tepid response to *City of Women* (1980), decided to discreetly visit cinemas in Rome to gauge audiences' reactions for himself. He discovered that 'the audience had changed planet, it no longer existed'.[30] This mournful assessment helps us understand the valedictory yet defiant tone of his last period.

After the success of *Amarcord*, the public lost interest in Fellini, even though the baroque excesses of the Felliniesque aesthetic had entered the mainstream. The media reduced him to his own caricature while his films were greeted with incomprehension, controversy or even indifference. In the period between *Fellini's Casanova* (1976) and *La voce della luna* (1990) Italian cinema went through a major creative crisis, mainly triggered by the emergence of 'neo-television'. The appearance of private TV channels — and that of Silvio Berlusconi's financial and political empire — led to a banalization of the image. This phenomenon was accompanied by a dearth of exemplars in Italian cinema: some directors were working abroad (Bertolucci and Antonioni), the old masters were dead (Rossellini, Pasolini, Visconti) and audiences were deserting

cinemas that had failed to keep up with the times. Ensconced within the studios of Cinecittà, Fellini would continue to create startling, visionary images, while resisting a society of spectacle that embraced television to the detriment of any artistic or intellectual standards.

Farewell to the male

At the start of *Fellini's Casanova*, the waters of the Grand Canal become the dreamlike setting for an imaginary Venice that gives birth to the splendid figure of Venus. This scene touches on two crucial points. On the one hand, Fellini drew on the carnival to paint a grandiose, symbolic picture of femininity, showing how an exploration of the myth of the eternal seducer can lead to a visionary construction of the female archetype, which would later be developed in the oneiric labyrinths of *City of Women*. On the other hand, there are clear links between Fellini's imaginary geography of Venice and the idea of invisible cities developed by Italo Calvino.[31] Fellini placed the Rialto alongside the Campanile in the Piazza San Marco and used plastic to depict the sea. From then on, the atmosphere of the film is spectral, in opposition to the empirical world. Any historiographic element is expressed

in 'inverted commas'. Fellini was more than ever a demiurge whose visual exaggeration serves as the basis for his imagined universes.

Fellini drew little inspiration from *Histoire de ma vie* (*History of My Life*), the memoirs in which Giacomo Girolamo Casanova described his wanderings from one European court to another in the late eighteenth century. Fellini viewed Casanova as a cadaverous puppet who had never really left his mother's womb and never stopped fantasizing as he passed through a world stripped of all emotions. The sexuality of this seducer is animal, he copulates like an automaton, like the mechanical bird that keeps him company. As played by Donald Sutherland, Casanova looks like a seahorse and is more ridiculous than anything else. The Europe through which he roams is an abstract continent, the quest for pleasure becomes an absence of life, the male sperm is as cold as that of a zombie.

Casanova is accused of being a freemason and is imprisoned in Venice's Piombi prison. He manages to escape, however, and goes from one phantasmagoric place to another: first the experimental surgery of Madame d'Urfé, who is intent on finding the secret to immortality, then the theatre of a homosexual hunchback named Du Bois, where the legend of the praying-mantis mistress is evoked, and, finally, while on the trail of a giantess who emerges from the River Thames in London, the belly of a whale. As in *Fellini Satyricon*, the characters seem to be moving among ghosts. Casanova is 'a machine devoted to the panoptic enjoyment of others, who works his body to satisfy the fantasy of omnipotence of other people, be they man or woman'.[32] This sexual athlete lives permanently on the frontier between life and death. At the end he achieves plenitude by becoming a puppet dancing with the only woman he is capable of loving — a mechanical doll.

The shoot for *Fellini's Casanova* was particularly arduous, the most difficult that Fellini had ever undertaken. It began in 1975, was interrupted, and eventually restarted in March 1976, after a deal with the producer Alberto Grimaldi. The film aroused great expectation in the media but proved to be a flop, despite the Oscar awarded to Danilo Donati for its sets and costumes.

Donald Sutherland in *Fellini's Casanova* (1976).

Making death visible
Fellini's Casanova

Fellini was always fascinated both by the mystery of death and the impossibility of capturing that mystery on screen. At the end of *8½* he considered filming the great beyond as a train journey but ended up substituting it with a parade celebrating life. He wanted to show a crash landing into the nothingness of death in *Il Viaggio di G. Mastorna* but the film was never made. And although in 'Toby Dammit' he did show the ritual inherent to dying, it was only in the last scene of *Fellini's Casanova* that he ventured beyond death.

In half-light, Casanova, his face marked by age, wonders: 'Will I go back to Venice one day?' A young Casanova, seen in wide shot, walks through a Venice shrouded in plastic ice. The large bust of the goddess Venus, the symbol of femininity that coincides with the full moon, seems to have been buried. Women come down some stairs, vanish and then reappear in front of an artificial Rialto.

A golden carriage comes into shot, bearing the Pope and a woman; they berate Casanova. He finds the mechanical doll, Rosalba, approaches her and starts to dance with her. Nino Rota's score suggests the sound of a music box. A close-up of Casanova's eyes makes it clear how much he has aged. In the great beyond, he continues to dance with the doll and turns into an inanimate object himself. In this way, Fellini leads us into a ghostly world where desire ices over, people become automatons and youth fades into eternity.

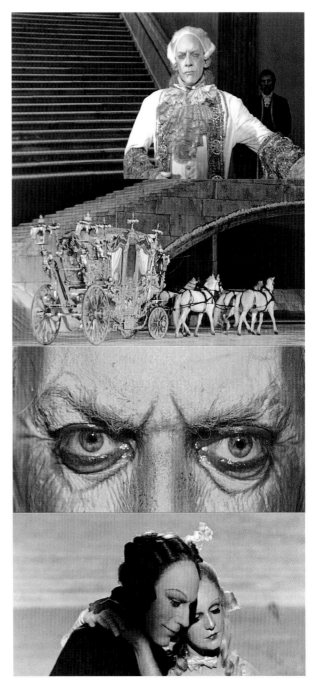

Donald Sutherland in *Fellini's Casanova* (1976).

Giacomo Casanova was revisited via the character of Dr. Xavier Katzone (Ettore Manni) in *City of Women*. Katzone — inspired by the writer Georges Simenon[33] — is a superman, one of a breed on the verge of extinction, and he has a mausoleum where he commemorates the high points of his life as a seducer. Into this world stumbles Snàporaz (Marcello Mastroianni), akin to the troubled, self-obsessed artist of *8½*. This time he finds himself embroiled in a dream in which his sexual desires manifest themselves in the form of multiple images of femininity. In a sense, *City of Women* is the opposite of *Fellini's Casanova*. Fellini creates a nightmare in which his double, Snàporaz, discovers that the death of the male leads to another reality in which the future is female. What is it like, this world dominated by women into which Snàporaz is catapulted? The man who pursues the object of his desire finds himself trapped in a huge feminists' convention in which the women are grouped into tribes: the maternal woman, the ideal woman and the sensual woman are in cahoots to pass judgement on men. At the convention, Snow White, now a dominatrix, exhibits her seven husbands. Snàporaz runs away, only to lose himself in the countless labyrinths of his own ego. He slides down on a toboggan, sees before him all his childhood memories and ends up face to face with the ideal woman. This scene is pure visual hyperbole, allowing Fellini to bring a masturbatory passion to his creation.

As in *Fellini's Casanova*, the male loses himself in the female jungle and ends up ensnared by an inanimate figure, in this case a large doll flying in an enormous hot-air balloon. *Fellini's Casanova* and *City of Women* are two hallucinatory explorations of femininity in which Fellini recorded the multiple images triggered in his unconscious by women and pushed his visionary capacities to new extremes.

Federico Fellini on the set of *City of Women* (1980).

Following pages: *City of Women* (1980).

Nino Rota

With many scores to his credit, Nino Rota (1911–1979) was a major figure in the story of film music. Although he worked with Luchino Visconti (*Rocco and His Brothers*, 1960; *The Leopard*, 1963), Francis Ford Coppola (*The Godfather*, 1972) and King Vidor (*War and Peace*, 1956), his name will always be associated with that of Fellini. The Rota–Fellini tandem collaborated on seventeen films, from *The White Sheik* to *Orchestra Rehearsal*. For Fellini, Rota rewrote popular melodies from the 1920s (*Amarcord*), circus fanfares (*The Clowns*, *8½*) and sentimental tunes (*La strada*), as well as creating more experimental scores inspired by baroque opera (*Fellini's Casanova*). Rota's music intensified still further Fellini's melancholic, dreamlike vision by continually moving between melodies that transformed the evocative power of the images and others that integrated perfectly into the narrative texture and heightened the atmosphere of Fellini's world. Music was also inextricably intertwined with key motifs in Fellini's work, most typically the catwalk parade, which inevitably recalls the circus. At the end of *8½*, all the characters form a procession; similarly, in *The White Sheik*, when Wanda arrives on the set for the photostory, the disguised characters emerge in a parade. In Fellini's films, the world seems to be one big show.

Federico Fellini, Shirley Verrett and Nino Rota in the 1970s.

Federico Fellini on the set of *Orchestra Rehearsal* (1978).

Following pages: *And the Ship Sails On* (1983).

The remains of the shipwreck

Between *Fellini's Casanova* and *City of Women*, Fellini shot *Orchestra Rehearsal* (1978) for RAI. Focusing on the rehearsals of a group of musicians in a chapel in Rome, Fellini asks them about their instruments and then establishes links between these instruments and the physical characteristics of the people who play them. Gradually, however, the film turns into a political fable about the discipline and power of artistic creation. The musicians rebel against the tyranny of the conductor but the super-ego, in the form of a gigantic ball, imposes order and ensures that the piece is eventually performed. *Orchestra Rehearsal* starts by recording a creative process — the performance of a piece of music — and ends up as a reflection on the search for harmony. This would be Fellini's last collaboration with Nino Rota, who died of a heart attack shortly afterwards.

After *City of Women* Fellini started to bury his world. Opera served him as a metaphor, as if it

had become a repository for the keys to the hyperbolic vision that his films had progressively come to embody. As an art form that tends toward pure imagination, opera bases the intensity of its spectacle on artifice and its overall unity on materials as diverse as music, stage design and drama. As Youssef Ishaghpour has written, when cinema and opera met in 1914, opera emerged debilitated and cinema was strengthened, as Hollywood appropriated opera's spectacular dimension.[34] This cinematic parasitism is depicted in the first scene of *And the Ship Sails On* (1983), when the transition from silent, black and white film to sound and colour is represented on screen, ushering in an elaborate film-opera, which was produced by Daniel Toscan du Plantier for Gaumont.

The film tells of a funeral and shipwreck in 1914. The funeral is that of the great diva Edmea Tetua, whose ashes are going to be scattered on an island in the Mediterranean. For this purpose, a group of decadents hire a ship that inevitably 81

Barbara Jefford (centre) in *And the Ship Sails On* (1983).

recalls the Ship of Fools.[35] These eccentric characters are deeply disturbing. They symbolize the end of the divine, of aristocratic exuberance and extravagant, nonsensical rituals. Their powerful operatic voices are drowned out in this age of hullabaloo: the singers have to perform their arias against the hellish racket of the ship's boilers. Nothing sublime can be discerned in the myth of grand opera, as it has evaporated in a popular culture fed by the media, represented here by a journalist who tries to make order out of the chaos. This narrator is another of Fellini's *alter egos*. Chiding the viewer, he hones in on one fixed idea: documenting the moment as it is lived. Everything is mere artifice, the ship itself is revealed as a set and the sea is made of plastic. The decadents encounter a group of Serbian refugees who announce the start of World War I. It is the end of an era.

The ship is destroyed, the only survivors being the narrator and a rhinoceros, a creature apparently surfacing from the story's unconscious. The symbolic shipwreck of these figures from the world of opera is indicative of a far more pervasive shipwreck. These people are caricatures created by Fellini, pathetic parodic faces that convey truths about the world through exaggeration. *And the Ship Sails On* is the first part of a shipwreck that would be continued with *Ginger and Fred* (1985) and *Fellini's Intervista* (1987), two melancholy films about the destruction of cinema by television.

The ruins of the spectacle

Amelia (Giulietta Masina) and Pippo (Marcello Mastroianni), the main characters in *Ginger and Fred*, are a couple of ghosts. Fellini's double — Marcello, Guido Anselmi, Snàporaz — and his wife, the embodiment of female otherness, make a

Marcello Mastroianni in *Ginger and Fred* (1985)   Following pages: Giulietta Masina and Marcello Mastroianni in *Ginger and Fred* (1985).

comeback to recapture an emotional bond in a confused and chaotic present. Marcello and Giulietta, Fellini and Masina, no longer develop separately — as they did in the key films of the past — but together, as vital fundaments of Fellini's creative universe. Time has left its mark, however: everything has been eroded. Now the two ghosts want to recover a little of what they have lost but they are no longer confronted by the real world, as that has been definitively eclipsed by spectacular representations. Copies, doubles and other palimpsests of the real inhabit the world that Amelia and Pippo have to negotiate. They are themselves just pieces in a game, not real people but imitators, doubles of Ginger Rogers and Fred Astaire. Over the course of the film, they come across doubles of Marcel Proust, Franz Kafka, Clark Gable and Woody Allen. They want to dance again, to re-create their plush but long-gone world of music hall — but the past

cannot be reached, as it is marooned in a monstrous present, and any attempt at reconciliation appears out of the question.

Ginger and Fred has the air of a Christmas story. Amelia and Pippo go to the TV studios on New Year's Eve to appear in a variety show. Their participation represents both a reunion and the discovery of the new technological circus known as television, which exploits the freaks of the age under its electronic big top and gives undue importance to the dregs of society. In the heart of this empire, everything seems condemned to derision. The popular revues of the *avanspettacolo* and the illusions of the circus, with their whiteface and auguste clowns, have given way to the world of the simulacrum, responsible for what Jean Baudrillard has called the 'perfect crime', the assassination of the real.[36] The exterior world — the rubbish on the streets, with the symbolic image of the Roma Termini railway

station set on an enormous pig's foot in the foreground — has become a cannibalistic space raised above the organic detritus of opulence.

Fellini paints a bitter picture of the power of this neo-television, the great audiovisual monster that has engulfed cinematic creation and at the same time imposed the rule of the false. Despite its apocalyptic tone, a tenderness on Fellini's part towards his characters — barely evident since *Amarcord* — seems to re-emerge in *Ginger and Fred*. Amelia and Pippo relive something intense, even though it is lost for ever. Fellini knows full well that the only solace in this new world of shadows is melancholic nostalgia. So, after this journey into the heart of the society of spectacle to observe the source of its machinations, he felt the need to return to Cinecittà, the one place where it was still possible to nurture his last illusions. *Ginger and Fred* also marked Fellini's reunion with his old friends Tullio Pinelli, the scriptwriter, and Franco Fabrizi, the lead in *I vitelloni* and *The Swindle*.

In one scene in *Fellini's Intervista* — a film constructed, like *Fellini's Roma*, around an alternation between the past and the present — Fellini remembers how the best way to get to Cinecittà in the 1940s was to follow the elephants. The young Fellini follows the road of illusion in a tram and arrives at Cinecittà to interview a diva. Like the circus of *The Clowns*, the studios were a place in which illusion was revealed. For him, like the young Orson Welles, they were the biggest electric train set in the world. Cinecittà was once the symbol of Fellini's empire, of the fiefdom in which he was the demiurge, but the studios are now under threat and the art of cinema is forced to rub shoulders with advertising. In *Fellini's Intervista*, it is in these studios that Fellini the creator receives journalists from Japanese television, tells them of the splendours of years gone by and expounds his theory of cinema as a process whereby the world is re-created.

Inside the Cinecittà studio, Fellini directs, as Guido Anselmi had done in *8½*, a film destined never to see the light of day: an adaptation of Franz Kafka's *Amerika*.[37] Stage hands paint the scenery while the assistant director looks for caricaturish faces that fit Fellini's world. *Fellini's Intervista* is a self-referential work of synthesis, a film in which the play of mirrors between fiction and reality, between a work and its development, is perfectly realized. It bears witness to a desire to remake *Fellini: A Director's Notebook*, resulting in a remarkable filmed essay.

Towards the end of the film, when the crew shelters from the rain under tarpaulins, danger appears in the form of a group of Indian people with TV antennas, highlighting the fact that the world over which Fellini once reigned is in the process of being taken over by an even more powerful empire: television.

While Fellini is conjuring up his world in *Fellini's Intervista*, Marcello Mastroianni appears once again. For the last time, the creator and his creature are on screen together. The evocation of the glorious Cinecittà of days long gone is counterpointed by the sight of its former splendours. Marcello looks back to the past only to meet up once again with Anita Ekberg, overweight and cruelly aged. The two of them watch the handsome Marcello and the exuberant Anita in the famous Trevi Fountain scene from *La Dolce Vita*. Nobody can return from the kingdom of the dead: cinema and youth belong to another age, the shipwreck has already taken place.

Plays of mirrors
Fellini's Intervista

At the beginning of *The Order of Things: An archaeology of the human sciences* (*Les Mots et les choses*, 1966), Michel Foucault remarks that the truly modern aspect of the painting of Velázquez is his substitution of representation for the system by which a subject is represented. In Fellini's films he projects himself onto one of his doubles to throw light on his own creative process. Sometimes – in *Fellini's Roma*, *The Clowns*, *Fellini's Intervista* and, to a certain extent, *Orchestra Rehearsal* – Fellini becomes a character himself and the film takes on the trappings of a documentary, showing a shoot where everything is controlled by the gaze of the demiurge.

There is a long scene in *Fellini's Intervista* in which Fellini pushes his Pirandellian game with the creative process to its extremes.

He reflects, with half an eye on posterity, on time past. The sequence begins with Fellini and his crew preparing the film that would never come to fruition, his adaptation of Kafka's *Amerika*. Marcello Mastroianni, disguised as Mandrake the Magician, appears at a window as if by magic. The real trick, however, is Fellini's baroque gesture of showing us his double and sharing the frame with him. The actor is neither Guido Anselmi nor Snàporaz nor Pippo – he is Marcello Mastroianni himself. On the sound stage where a commercial is being shot, Fellini introduces Sergio Rubini to Marcello. In *Fellini's Intervista* this young actor is the double of the young Fellini. The creator appears surrounded by his creatures, and the three of them get into the back of a car. They leave Cinecittà to travel through the suburbs

– the no man's land beloved of Fellini – accompanied by the new paparazzi from Japanese TV. They stop at the Villa Pandora. During the journey, Fellini's doubles hide him from view, allowing him to stay in the shadows and operate as a master creator.

Anita Ekberg lives in the Villa Pandora. She appears wrapped in a towel, as if irrevocably destined to remain a mermaid. She is surrounded by her dogs. The young Rubini sees her as a diva but Marcello watches her sadly: her bloated figure confirms the passing of time in the cruellest of ways. She offers her guests wine and sweet chestnuts. Mandrake–Marcello makes a screen appear as if by magic. Nino Rota's music from *La Dolce Vita* starts playing and the magician invokes the past: the screen becomes the mirror of what has been lost

– the young journalist Marcello dances with the sensual Swedish star in the cabaret scene in *La Dolce Vita*. Anita falls under the spell of nostalgia, brusquely dispelled by a sarcastic Marcello asking for a glass of grappa, to remind him of the good old days. Anita frolics in the waters of the Trevi Fountain and Marcello asks her if she is a goddess, a mother or Eve herself. Fellini, his doubles, the ideal woman and the images of the past are nothing more than mirror images. This scene illustrates that the condition of cinema is that of a spectral art capable of preserving lost time.

Federico Fellini, Sergio Rubini, Marcello Mastroianni and Anita Ekberg in *Fellini's Intervista* (1987).

Following pages: *Fellini's Intervista* (1987).

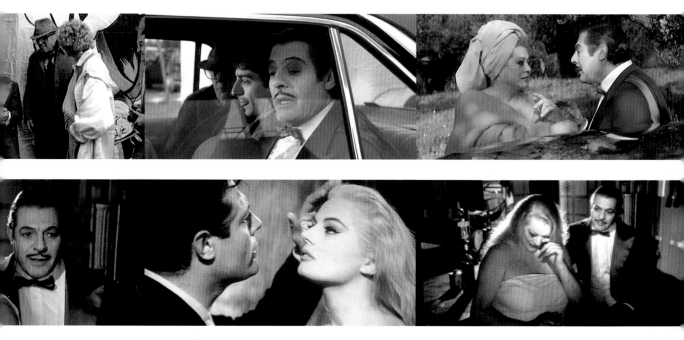

'Thoth, Fellini and the Pharaoh', by Umberto Eco

It goes without saying that Fellini is above all a man of cinema. And we often hear that, despite unquestionably being an art form, cinema – a means of expression as young today as writing was in the time of the pharaohs – is the art that forges most links with external reality. Obviously, when the *auteur* invents, he does so on the basis of what reality provides him: people, landscapes, colours and sounds.

And if reality is absent, then cinema, instead of making a story out of it, has to re-create it or, more precisely, stage it. Even if the landscapes are papier mâché and the characters are made of aluminium (like the robot in *Star Wars*, 1977), what is important is to create something pre-filmic, something which, before being recorded (or rather deformed) by the camera and editing, has belonged to materiality, organicity, three-dimensional reality. Far be it for me to raise all these questions, which are probably those of a naive beginner, especially as renowned theorists have already spoken with great conviction about cinema and the 'semiology of reality' – I am thinking particularly of Pier Paolo Pasolini, who has defended these arguments zealously, right to the hilt. Without any doubt, I shall say that Federico Fellini is a filmmaker who has ceaselessly reiterated in all his films, from the first to the last, from the most successful to the most disdained, that cinema (ambiguously caught up in the recording of exterior reality) is above all an art of memory. Our memories, our ghosts and our obsessions can always be explained via the fundaments of this art.

Obviously, one could say the same about other directors but Fellini is the one who has obstinately gone the furthest in this respect. As if he had lived to redeem the cinema from what is external to it, from pre-filmic reality, to show us that such a reality, despite all the traces it leaves on the world, is ultimately of the order of invention. And it is therefore possible to envisage an art that is above all the reconstruction of inner worlds, however private they may be. In this sense, the expression 'amarcord' is not just the title of one of his films, it is also the title of his *opus magnum*.

Triply majestic, like the god Thoth, Fellini on his vessel has always wanted to go beyond what this exterior world has tried to impose on his interiority and his voracity for nostalgia.

This is an extract from Umberto Eco, 'Theut, Fellini e il faraone' in Ester Carla de Miro d'Ajeta and Mario Guaraldi (eds.), *Fellini della memoria*, La Casa Usher, Florence, 1983.

Sim (right) in *La voce della luna* (1990).

Opposite page: Federico Fellini with Roberto Benigni on the set of *La voce della luna* (1990).

Silence

Having buried his world of carnival and caricature, having witnessed cinema in its death throes,
Fellini plunged into nostalgia as a means of escape
and decided to revisit one of his earliest arche-
types: the naive dreamer, the lunatic (in the original sense of the word) touched with madness. He
wanted to see if it was still possible to create a little
poetry amid the uproar of the modern world. *La voce
della luna* (1990), inspired by Ermanno Cavazzoni's
Poema dei lunatici, is a desperate attempt to seek
harmony in the confusion of the present day. The
main character, Ivo Salvini (Roberto Benigni), is
captivated by voices that speak to him from the

bottoms of wells. He wanders fitfully through a provincial town in which any trace of the past capable of awakening memories has been erased. He meets other simpletons who share his indifference to the real world and suspect, like him, that the visible merely obscures a huge farce. At first, Ivo — like Fellini the visionary, the visionary he had been from the start — searches for a reality hidden behind what we think we see, but, despite his poetic soliloquies, he does not succeed. Ivo is condemned to see the ideal woman through a peephole and observe how the social immaturity of his country means that there is always somebody crazy enough to shoot the moon.

In *La voce della luna* something seems to be irretrievably broken. The town consists of pieces of other possible towns. The attempt to recover childhood via the character of a sensual grandmother is futile. The provincial rituals, such as the Miss Flour contest, are pathetic, and events such as the entrapment of the moon in a garage are broadcast live on an all-seeing television screen that filters out all reality. In the centre of this chaotic realm, pounded by the deafening noise of a discothèque where violins were once played, Fellini decided to put a full stop to his career by pleading for silence as a means to aspire to greater understanding between human beings. This would be his final testament.

Presented out of competition at Cannes, without Fellini's presence, *La voce della luna* met with little commercial success, while some critics accused its maker of regurgitating visual motifs without the inspiration of the old. On 29 March 1993, Fellini received an honorary Oscar in Hollywood and on 28 June, during a brief trip to Rimini, he had a stroke. On 1 October, with the left side of his body paralysed, he was hospitalized in Rome, where Giulietta Masina was already languishing with cancer. He died on 31 October; his coffin was laid out in Studio 5 in Cinecittà and 60,000 people came to pay their last respects. On 23 March of the following year, Giulietta Masina died.

Chronology

1920

Born 20 January, the first child of Ida Barbiani and Urbano Fellini. The following year his brother Riccardo was born, followed by his sister Maddalena in 1929.

1925

A pupil at the school of the Sisters of San Vicenzo, before going to the Teatini primary school.

1930

Enrols in the Gimnasio Liceo-Giulio Cesare, situated alongside the Grand Hotel in Rimini. One of his classmates is Luigi Benzi, better known as Titta, who becomes a close friend; he would go on to be a major source of inspiration for the main character in *Amarcord*.

1936

Draws a series of caricatures of participants in a Fascist party youth camp in Verucchio.

1937

Carlo Massa, the owner of the Fulgor cinema, commissions him to draw a series of caricatures of American actors to attract audiences.

1938

Publishes humorous drawings in the weekly publication *La Domenica del Corriere* and contributes to the political and satirical weekly *Nerbini*, published in Florence.

1939

Arrives in Rome. Enrols in the university, as a law student, but does not get his degree. He starts working for the humorous twice-weekly publication *Marc'Aurelio* and continues until 1942. Through the comedian Ruggero Maccari, he meets Aldo Fabrizi. He starts to work as a gag writer for variety shows and cinema.

1940

Italy enters the war. He works on comedy shows for the radio. He creates gags for the film *The Pirate's Dream* (*Il pirata sono io!*), directed by Mario Mattoli.

1942

Meets Giulietta Masina, whom he marries on 30 October 1943. While working in the offices of the Alleanza Cinematografica Italiana (ACI), the company run by Vittorio Mussolini (son of Benito Mussolini, Il Duce), he meets Roberto Rossellini.

1943

Collaborates on the scripts for Mario Bonnard's *Peddler and the Lady* (*Campo dei Fiori*) and Mario Mattoli's *The Last Wagon* (*L'ultima carrozzella*). Allied troops land in Sicily.

1944

After the liberation of Rome, he opens the Funny Face Shop, where he draws portraits and caricatures. Roberto Rossellini asks him to work on a project about the execution by the SS of the priest Don Giuseppe Morosini. This results in him working on the screenplay for *Rome, Open City*, alongside Sergio Amidei.

1945

On 22 March his son is born, but dies after only two weeks due to respiratory difficulties.

1946

Participates in the scriptwriting and preparation for Roberto Rossellini's *Paisan*. Directs some shots for the episode set in Florence.

1947

Works as a screenwriter on some key films in Italian cinema of the time, such as Alberto Lattuada's *Flesh Will Surrender* (*Il delitto di Giovanni Episcopo*) and *Senza pietà*.

1948

Acts in 'Il miracolo', one of two episodes comprising *L'amore*, directed by Roberto Rossellini. He collaborates on the screenplays for Pietro Germi's *In the Name of the Law* (*In nome della legge*) and Alberto Lattuada's *The Mill on the Po* (*Il mulino del Po*).

1949

Collaborates on the writing and shooting of Roberto Rossellini's *The Flowers of St. Francis* (*Francesco, giullare di Dio*).

1950

Collaborates on the screenplay for Pietro Germi's *Path of Hope* (*Il cammino della speranza*). Co-directs *Variety Lights* with Alberto Lattuada.

1951

Collaborates on the screenplays for Roberto Rossellini's *Europa '51* and Pietro Germi's *Four Ways Out* (*La città si difende*) and *Il brigante di Tacca del Lupo*. Shoots his first film as sole director, *The White Sheik*, which also marks his first collaboration with Nino Rota.

1953

Wins the Silver Lion at the Venice Film Festival for *I vitelloni*. Shoots the short 'Agenzia matrimoniale' for the anthology film *Love in the City*.

1954

Shoots *La strada*, his first big popular success. It wins the Silver Lion at Venice and marks the beginning of a major international career.

1955

Shoots *The Swindle*.

1956

Wins his first Oscar in the category of best foreign film for *La strada*. Shoots *Nights of Cabiria*.

1957

Wins his second Oscar for *Nights of Cabiria*. Death of his father, Urbano Fellini. This loss gives rise to the screenplay *Viaggio con Anita*, co-written with Tullio Pinelli. The project did not bear fruit until it was taken up in 1979 by Mario Monicelli.

1959

Shoots *La Dolce Vita*.

The theatre Fulgor in Rimini in the 1940s.

Roberto Rossellini, Federico Fellini and Giulietta Masina during the shooting of Robert Rossellini's *Paisan* (1946).

Federico Fellini with producer Dino de Laurentiis on the set of *Nights of Cabiria* (1957).

Shooting of *8½* (1963).

Wins the Palme d'Or at the Cannes Film Festival for *La Dolce Vita*. Nominated for the Academy Awards, *La Dolce Vita* wins its only Oscar for best costumes (by Piero Gherardi).

1961

Shoots 'The Temptation of Dr. Antonio' for the anthology film *Boccaccio '70*. Meets the psychoanalyst Ernst Bernhard, who introduces him to the theories of Jung.

1962

Shoots *8½*.

1964

Wins his third Oscar for *8½*, and Piero Gherardi wins his second Oscar for the costumes.

1965

Shoots *Juliet of the Spirits*. Takes LSD under medical supervision. Writes the screenplay for *Il Viaggio di G. Mastorna* with Dino Buzzati.

1967

Nearly dies after a heart attack and stays in hospital for several months. Gives up on *Il Viaggio di G. Mastorna*. Writes the autobiographical text *La mia Rimini*. Shoots 'Toby Dammit' for the anthology film *Spirits of the Dead*.

1968

Shoots *Fellini: A Director's Notebook* for the American TV channel NBC.

1969

Shoots *Fellini Satyricon*, which is freely inspired by Petronius' eponymous book.

1970

Plays himself in Paul Mazursky's film *Alex in Wonderland*. Directs *The Clowns* for RAI.

1971

Shoots *Fellini's Roma*, with locations reconstructed in the Cinecittà studios.

1972

Shoots *Amarcord*.

1974

Wins the Oscar for best foreign film with *Amarcord*, a big international success. Plays himself in *C'eravamo tanto amati*, directed by Ettore Scola.

1975

Laborious and expensive shooting of *Fellini's Casanova* in the Cinecittà studios.

1977

Fellini's Casanova released, to a disappointing reception. Prepares *City of Women*.

1978

Shoots *Orchestra Rehearsal* for RAI. It is previewed to an audience of Italy's top political figures in the Quirinal Palace in Rome. The film provokes a stormy political debate.

1979

Death of his longtime collaborator Nino Rota. Shoots *City of Women*, which is greeted frostily by some critics.

1980

Publishes his book *Fare un film* with Einaudi.

1982

Shoots *And the Ship Sails On*, a co-production with French companies as a result of the general crisis in Italian cinema and consequent difficulties in raising financial backing. The film proved a critical success.

1983

Plays himself in Alberto Sordi's *Il tassinaro*.

1984

Shoots a commercial for Campari. Death of Ida Barbiani, his mother. Meets the writer Carlos Castaneda in Mexico.

1985

Shoots *Ginger and Fred*. Battles against Silvio Berlusconi's television empire. Has another heart attack. Receives the Venice Film Festival's Golden Lion for lifetime achievement.

1986

Shoots *Fellini's Intervista*.

1987

Publishes 'Viaggio a Tulum', an account of his experiences with Carlos Castaneda, in the *Corriere della sera*. Shoots a commercial for Barilla. *Fellini's Intervista* is warmly received at the Cannes Film Festival.

1988

Publishes his book *Un regista a Cinecittà* with Mondadori.

1989

Shoots his last film, *La voce della luna*.

1990

Receives the Praemium Imperiale in Tokyo. Presentation of *La voce della luna* in Cannes, to a negative reaction from critics.

1991

Fights against a law authorizing television channels to insert advertising breaks in films. Oversees Milo Manara's comic-strip realization of *Viaggio a Tulum*.

1992

Works with Milo Manara again, on a comic-strip adaptation of *Il Viaggio di G. Mastorna*. Shoots a commercial for the Bank of Rome.

1993

Receives an Oscar for lifetime achievement. Has a stroke in Rimini in June. Suffers a second stroke in Rome, where he dies on 31 October. A memorial service is held in Studio 5 at Cinecittà.

1994

Giulietta Masina dies on 23 March.

Federico Fellini on the set of *Fellini Satyricon* (1969).

Federico Fellini on the set of *Orchestra Rehearsal* (1978).

Federico Fellini on the set of *Amarcord* (1973).

Federico Fellini on the set of *Fellini's Intervista* (1987).

Federico Fellini on the set of *La voce della luna* (1990).

Filmography

ACTOR ONLY

'Il miracolo' 1948
by Roberto Rossellini
Alex in Wonderland 1970
by Paul Mazursky
**We All Loved
Each Other So Much** 1974
by Ettore Scola
Il tassinaro 1983
by Alberto Sordi

SHORT FILMS

'Agenzia matrimoniale' 1953
Running time 16 mins. With Antonio
Cifariello, Lidia Venturini.
• A young journalist reports on marriage agencies. Fourth episode of
Love in the City (*L'amore in città*).
**'The Temptation
of Dr. Antonio'** 1962
*Le tentazioni
del dottor Antonio*
Running time 54 mins. With Peppino
De Filippo, Anita Ekberg.
• Dr. Antonio is upset because a
large billboard featuring a highly
sensual woman extolling the virtues
of milk has just been put up opposite his home. Second episode of
Boccaccio '70.
'Toby Dammit' 1968
*Toby Dammit
o Non scommettere
la testa col diavolo*
Running time 37 mins. With Terence
Stamp, Salvo Randone, Antonia
Pietrosi.
• Toby Dammit is an American actor
who travels to Rome. His journey
turns into a spectral trip towards
death. Third episode of *Spirits of
the Dead*.

TELEVISION FILMS

**Fellini: A Director's
Notebook** 1968
*Block-notes
di un regista*
Running time 60 mins. With
Federico Fellini, Giulietta Masina,
Marcello Mastroianni, Caterina
Boratto, Marina Boratto.
• In front of the set for *Il Viaggio di
G. Mastorna*, Fellini reflects on the
abandoned film and on the one he
now wants to make: *Fellini Satyricon*.
The Clowns 1970
I clowns
Running time 1h 33. With Federico
Fellini, Liana Orfei, Franco Migliorini,
Anita Ekberg, Tristan Rémy and
Charlie Rivel.
• Fellini the boy discovers the circus
and the magic of clowns in Rimini.
Fellini the adult shoots a documentary about the death of the circus.

FEATURE FILMS

Variety Lights 1950
Luci del varietà
B&W. **Co-director** Alberto Lattuada. **Screenplay** Federico Fellini,
Alberto Lattuada, Tullio Pinelli, with
the collaboration of Ennio Flaiano,
from an idea by Federico Fellini. **Cinematography** Otello Martelli. **Production design** Aldo Buzzi. **Editing** Mario Bonotti. **Music** Felice
Lattuada. **Producers** Bianca Lattuada, Federico Fellini. **Production** Capitolium Films. **Running
time** 1h 40. With Carla Del Poggio
(Liliana 'Lilly' Antonelli), Peppino De
Filippo (Checco Dalmonte), Giulietta
Masina (Melina Amour).
• Liliana joins a small travelling theatre
company, but the director, Checco,
becomes jealous of her great success. She is eventually offered a
contract in Rome, but the rest of the
company has to continue touring.

The White Sheik 1952
Lo sceicco bianco
B&W. **Screenplay** Federico Fellini, Tullio Pinelli, from an idea by
Michelangelo Antonioni. **Cinematography** Arturo Gallea. **Production design** Raffaello Tolfo. **Editing** Rolando Benedetti. **Music** Nino
Rota. **Production** Luigi Rovere.
Running time 1h 25. With Alberto
Sordi (Fernando Rivoli), Brunella
Bovo (Wanda Giardino), Leopoldo
Trieste (Ivan Cavalli).
• Wanda and Ivan are in Rome on
honeymoon. She is fascinated by
show business and wanders off
onto a shoot for a photo-story, in
search of a fictional hero.

I vitelloni 1953
B&W. **Screenplay** Federico Fellini,
Ennio Flaiano, from an idea by Tullio
Pinelli. **Cinematography** Otello
Martelli, Luciano Trasatti, Carlo Carlini. **Production design** Mario Chiari.
Editing Rolando Benedetti. **Music**
Nino Rota. **Producer** Luigi Giacosi.

Production PEG-Film Cité Film.
Running time 1h 43. With Franco
Interlenghi (Moraldo), Alberto Sordi
(Alberto), Franco Fabrizi (Fausto),
Leopoldo Trieste (Leopoldo), Riccardo Fellini (Riccardo).
• In a small provincial city, five friends
while away the time in a café. Fausto
is married but is a womanizer, Alberto
is eaten up by his complexes and
Leopoldo dreams of being a celebrated poet.

La strada 1954
B&W. **Screenplay** Federico Fellini, Tullio Pinelli, with the collaboration of Ennio Flaiano. **Cinematography** Otello Martelli. **Production
design** Mario Ravasco. **Editing**
Leo Catozzo. **Music** Nino Rota.
Production Dino De Laurentiis,
Carlo Ponti **Running time** 1h 34.
With Giulietta Masina (Gelsomina),
Anthony Quinn (Zampanò), Richard
Basehart (The Fool).
• The uncouth Zampanò buys Gelsomina, an ignorant young simpleton. One day she meets the Fool, an
acrobat who constantly stands up
to Zampanò. After a confrontation,
Zampanò kills the Fool. Gelsomina
is devastated.

The Swindle 1955
Il bidone
B&W. **Screenplay** Federico Fellini,
Tullio Pinelli, Ennio Flaiano, with the
collaboration of Brunello Rondi. **Cinematography** Otello Martelli. **Production design** Dario Cecchi. **Editing** Mario Serandrei, Giuseppe Vari.
Music Nino Rota. **Production** Titanus, SGC. **Running time** 1h 44. With
Broderick Crawford (Augusto), Richard Basehart (Picasso), Franco Fabrizi (Roberto), Giulietta Masina (Iris).
• Three seedy conmen – Augusto,
Picasso and Roberto – disguise
themselves as priests to rob from
the poor.

Nights of Cabiria 1957
Le notti di Cabiria

B&W. **Screenplay** Federico Fellini. Adaptation of dialogues into Roman dialect by Pier Paolo Pasolini. **Cinematography** Aldo Tonti, Otello Martelli. **Production and costume design** Piero Gherardi. **Editing** Leo Cattozo. **Music** Nino Rota. **Producer** Dino De Laurentiis. **Production** Cinematografica, Roma and Films Marceau. **Running time** 1h 50. With Giulietta Masina (Cabiria), François Périer (Oscar D'Onofrio), Franca Marzi (Wanda), Dorian Gray (Jessy), Amedeo Nazzari (Alberto Lazzari).

• Cabiria is a prostitute who dreams of love. She meets an actor who rejects her and also meets Oscar, a young man who seems to be won over by her good nature.

La Dolce Vita 1960

B&W. **Screenplay** Federico Fellini, Tullio Pinelli, Ennio Flaiano. **Cinematography** Otello Martelli. **Production and costume design** Piero Gherardi. **Editing** Leo Catozzo. **Music** Nino Rota. **Producer** Giuseppe Amato. **Production** Riama Film, Roma, Gray Films, Pathé Consortium Cinéma. **Running time** 2h 58. With Marcello Mastroianni (Marcello Rubini), Anita Ekberg (Sylvia), Anouk Aimée (Maddalena), Magali Noël (Fanny), Lex Barker (Robert), Alain Cuny (Steiner), Annibale Ninchi (Marcello's father), Yvonne Furneaux (Emma).

• Marcello is a trendy journalist in Rome. He travels around the city and meets a Hollywood star, his provincial father and an intellectual who ends up killing his children.

8½ 1963
Otto e mezzo

B&W. **Screenplay** Federico Fellini, Tullio Pinelli, Ennio Flaian, Brunello Rondi. **Cinematography** Gianni Di Venanzo. **Production and costume design** Piero Gherardi. **Editing** Leo

Catozzo. **Music** Nino Rota. **Producers** Angelo Rizzoli, Federico Fellini. **Production** Cineriz, Francinex. **Running time** 1h 54. With Marcello Mastroianni (Guido Anselmi), Anouk Aimée (Luisa), Sandra Milo (Carla), Claudia Cardinale (Claudia), Rossella Falk (Rossella), Barbara Steele (Gloria), Edra Gale (La Saraghina).

• Guido is going through a serious creative crisis. While looking for a source of inspiration for his next film, he is haunted by his memories, dreams, demons and hallucinations.

Juliet of the Spirits 1965
Giulietta degli spiriti

Screenplay Federico Fellini, Tullio Pinelli, Ennio Flaiano. **Cinematography** Gianni Di Venanzo. **Production and costume design** Piero Gherardi. **Editing** Ruggero Mastroianni. **Music** Nino Rota. **Production** Angelo Rizzoli. **Running time** 2h 09. With Giulietta Masina (Giulietta), Sandra Milo (Susy, Iris, Fanny), Mario Pisu (Giorgio), Valentina Cortese (Valentina).

• Giulietta lives an unimpeachable middle-class life. Her husband cheats on her and she tries to come to terms with her repressed demons.

Fellini Satyricon 1969
Satyricon

Screenplay Federico Fellini, Bernardino Zapponi, with the collaboration of Brunello Rondi, freely adapted from Petronius. **Cinematography** Giuseppe Rotunno. **Production design** Danilo Donati. **Editing** Ruggero Mastroianni. **Music** Nino Rota. **Producer** Alberto Grimaldi. **Production** PEA (Rome) and United Artists (Paris). **Running time** 2h 18. With Martin Potter (Encolpio), Hiram Keller (Ascilto), Max Born (Gitone), Mario Romagnoli (Trimalcione), Magali Noël (Fortunata).

• Encolpio is despondent when his lover Gitone leaves with his friend Ascilto. His loss, his search for Gitone and his encounter with his rival are stages on a journey through a decadent Rome.

Fellini's Roma 1972
Roma

Screenplay Federico Fellini, Bernardino Zapponi. **Cinematography** Giuseppe Rotunno. **Production design** Danilo Donati. **Editing** Ruggero Mastroianni. **Music** Nino Rota. **Producer** Turi Vasile. **Production** Ultra Film and SPA (Rome), Productions Artistes Associés (Paris). **Running time** 1h 59. With Peter Gonzales (Fellini), Fiona Florence (Dolores), Marne Maitland (Guide to the catacombs).

• In a school in Rimini, the teacher tells stories about ancient Rome. The young Fellini arrives in Rome before the war and discovers its theatres and brothels. Fellini the filmmaker shoots a documentary about the city that focuses on the unseen Rome.

Amarcord 1973

Screenplay Federico Fellini, Tonino Guerra, after an idea by Federico Fellini. **Cinematography** Giuseppe Rotunno. **Production design** Danilo Donati. **Editing** Ruggero Mastroianni. **Music** Nino Rota. **Producer** Franco Cristaldi. **Production** FC Produzioni (Rome) and PECF (Paris). **Running time** 2h 07. With Bruno Zanin (Titta Biondi), Pupella Maggio (Titta's mother), Armando Brancia (Titta's father), Stefano Proietti (Titta's brother), Magali Noël (Gradisca).

• Chronicle of a year in the small provincial city of Rimini, on the Adriatic coast. Political life is dominated by Fascism and teenagers indulge in sexual fantasies.

Fellini's Casanova 1976
Il Casanova di Federico Fellini

Screenplay Federico Fellini, Bernardino Zapponi, after Giacomo Casanova's *History of My Life*. **Cinematography** Giuseppe Rotunno. **Production and costume design**

Danilo Donati. **Editing** Ruggero Mastroianni. **Music** Nino Rota. **Producer** Alberto Grimaldi **Production** PEA, Rome. **Running time** 2h 50 (Italy), 2h 30 (UK). With Donald Sutherland (Giacomo Casanova), Margaret Clementi (Sister Maria Maddalena), Cicely Browne (Madame d'Urfó), Tina Aumont (Henriette).

• Giacomo Casanova is imprisoned in Venice for his debauchery. He escapes and travels from one European court to another.

Orchestra Rehearsal 1978
Prova d'orchestra

Screenplay Federico Fellini, Bernardino Zapponi, with the collaboration of Brunello Rondi. **Cinematography** Giuseppe Rotunno. **Production design** Dante Ferretti. **Editing** Ruggero Mastroianni. **Music** Nino Rota. **Production** RAI and Albatros Produktion Gmbh. **Running time** 1h 10. With Balduin Baas (Conductor), Clara Colosimo (Harpist), Elizabeth Labi (Pianist), Federico Fellini (Voice of the interviewer).

• During the course of a rehearsal, a group of musicians rebel against the tyranny of their conductor.

City of Women 1980
La città delle donne

Screenplay Federico Fellini, Bernardino Zapponi, Brunello Rondi. **Cinematography** Giuseppe Rotunno. **Production design** Dante Ferretti. **Editing** Ruggero Mastroianni. **Music** Luis Bacalov. **Production** Opera F. Viva Int., Gaumont. **Running time** 2h 25. With Marcello Mastroianni (Snàporaz), Ettore Manni (Katzone), Anna Prucnal (Snàporaz's wife), Bernice Stegers (Woman on the train).

• A man on a train journey dreams that he desires a woman. Lost in a dream world, he comes upon a place entirely dominated by women.

And the Ship Sails On 1983
E la nave va
Screenplay Federico Fellini, Tonino Guerra. **Cinematography** Giuseppe Rotunno. **Production design** Dante Ferretti. **Editing** Ruggero Mastroianni. **Music** Gianfranco Plenizio. **Production** RAI, Vides Produzione and Gaumont. **Running time** 2h 12. With Freddie Jones (Orlando), Barbara Jefford (Ildebranda Cuffari), Victor Poletti (Aureliano Fuciletto), Peter Cellier (Sir Reginald Dongby), Pina Bausch (La Principessa Lherimia).
• At the start of the Great War several people from the world of opera set sail on board a ship to scatter at sea the ashes of a diva.

Ginger and Fred 1985
Ginger e Fred
Screenplay Federico Fellini, Tonino Guerra, Tullio Pinelli. **Cinematography** Tonino Delli Colli, Ennio Guarnieri. **Production design** Dante Ferretti. **Editing** Nino Baragli, Ugo De Rossi, Ruggero Mastroianni. **Music** Nicolà Piovani. **Production** Alberto Grimaldi. **Running time** 1h 43. With Giulietta Masina (Amelia), Marcello Mastroianni (Pippo), Franco Fabrizi (The Presenter).
• Amelia and Pippo are reunited after several years apart to impersonate, once again, Ginger Rogers and Fred Astaire on a television show.

Fellini's Intervista 1987
Intervista
Screenplay Federico Fellini, Gianfranco Angelucci. **Cinematography** Tonino Delli Colli. **Production design** Danilo Donati. **Editing** Nino Baragli. **Music** Nicolà Piovani. **Producer** Ibrahim Moussa. **Production** Aljosha Produccions, RAI and Cinecittà. **Running time** 1h 53. With Sergio Rubini (Young Fellini), Maurizio Mein (Assistant Director), Lara Wendel (The Bride), Federico Fellini, Anita Ekberg and Marcello Mastroianni as themselves.

• Fellini answers questions from Japanese journalists while preparing an adaptation of Kafka's *Amerika* in the Cinecittà studios.

La voce della luna 1990
Screenplay Federico Fellini, Tullio Pinelli, Ermanno Cavazzoni, freely adapted from *Il poema dei lunatici* by Ermanno Cavazzoni. **Cinematography** Tonino Delli Colli. **Production design** Dante Ferretti. **Editing** Nino Baragli. **Music** Nicolà Piovani. **Production** Cecchi Gori, RAI Uno. **Running time** 1h 58. With Roberto Benigni (Ivo Salvini), Paolo Villaggio (Gonnella), Marisa Tomasi (Marisa), Nadia Ottaviani (Aldina).
• Ivo Salvini hears strange voices emanating from a well. These voices guide him to a town where a man ends up trapping the moon and locking it in his garage.

Selected Bibliography

Books by Federico Fellini
Federico Fellini: The Films, ed. Tullio Kezich, Rizzoli, New York, 2010.

The Book of Dreams, ed. Tullio Kezich and Vittorio Boarini, Rizzoli, New York, 2008.

Federico Fellini: Interviews, ed. Bert Cardullo, University Press of Mississippi, Jackson, MS, 2006.

I'm a Born Liar: A Fellini Lexicon, ed. Damian Pettigrew, Harry N. Abrams, New York, 2003.

Fellini on Fellini, Da Capo Press, Cambridge, MA, 1996

Trip to Tulum (with Milo Manara), NBM Publishing, New York, 1996.

Cinecittà, tr. Graham Fawcett, Studio Vista, London, 1989.

Comments on Film, ed. Giovanni Grazzini, tr. Joseph Henry, The Press at California State University, Fresno, CA, 1988.

Fellini's Faces: 418 pictures from the photo-archives of Federico Fellini, ed. Christian Strich, Holt, Rinehart and Winston, Austin, TX, 1982.

Books about Federico Fellini
John Baxter, *Fellini*, Fourth Estate, London, 1993.

Peter Bondanella, *Federico Fellini*, Essays in Criticism, Oxford University Press, Oxford, 1978.

Peter Bondanella, *The Cinema of Federico Fellini*, with a foreword by Federico Fellini, Princeton University Press, Princeton NJ, 1992.

Tullio Kezich, *Federico Fellini: His Life and Work*, tr. Minna Proctor, I.B. Tauris, London, 2007.

Notes

1. The concept of 'neo-television' was created by Umberto Eco to define the type of television, based on privatization and the proliferation of channels, that appeared in Italy in the late 1970s. Its opposite is 'paleo-television', which consists exclusively of public service channels. See Umberto Eco, 'TV: la trasparenza perduta' in *Sette anni di desiderio*, Bompiani, Milan, 1983, p. 163.

2. Italian post-war cinema aimed to focus above all on the real. Two branches of neo-realism emerged: Marxist directors, headed by Luchino Visconti, who considered that cinema should present an analysis of reality by modernizing the techniques of the nineteenth-century novel; and the branch headed by Roberto Rossellini, who thought that cinema should explore the ways in which reality is understood and question its limits. Fellini, like Michelangelo Antonioni, sided with the latter tendency.

3. Federico Fellini, *Fare un film*, ET Saggi, Turin, 2006.

4. The screenwriter Ruggero Maccari started to work on *Marc'Aurelio* at the same time as Fellini. Aldo Fabrizi was then one of the top stars in variety.

5. Vittorio Mussolini (1916–97) founded the magazine *Cinema*, the principal arena for theoretical debates about neo-realism.

6. *Rome, Open City* (1945) was shot under precarious conditions, as the war had left the film industry in a parlous state. The film denounced the barbarities of Nazism and allowed the Italian cinema to make a committed stand with respect to the historical upheavals of World War II.

7. Pietro Germi (1914–74) and Alberto Lattuada (1914–2005) were key directors in Italian neo-realist cinema.

8. Tullio Kezich, *Fellini*, Rizzoli, Milan, 1988, p. 123.

9. Gianni Rondolino, 'Fellini e Rossellini: influenze reciproche', *Quaderni del CSCI: Rivista annuale di cinema italiano*, Istituto Italiano di Cultura, Barcelona, 2005, p. 105.

10. André Bazin (1918–58), a cofounder of *Cahiers du cinéma*, regarded cinema as a means to reproduce the real, and considered that it had emerged, historically speaking, as an extension of photography. Cinema was thus different, according to him, from representative arts that copied or imitated reality. Nevertheless, if reality were to be understood, its ambiguity had to be preserved and its mysteries revealed.

11. Jacqueline Risset, Fellini, *Le Cheik Blanc: L'annonce faite à Federico*, Adam Biro, Paris, 1990, p. 25.

12. Cesare Zavattini (1902–89) was one of Italy's top screenwriters and one of the main theorists of neo-realism. His name is inextricably linked to that of Vittorio De Sica, most notably on account of his screenplays for *Bicycle Thieves* (1948) and *Umberto D.* (1952). Zavattini believed that representing reality involves showing intimacy and capturing the real time of events. He conceived *Love in the City* (1953) as a 'magazine article' covering love in an urban context. The film comprises six episodes, directed, respectively, by Carlo Lizzani, Michelangelo Antonioni, Dino Risi, Federico Fellini, Cesare Zavattini and Francesco Maselli, and Alberto Lattuada.

13. André Bazin, 'Cabiria ou le voyage au bout du néoréalisme', *Cahiers du cinéma*, 76 (November 1957).

14. *Commedia dell'arte* takes as its starting point a series of stock characters – Harlequin, Columbine, Pantalone, etc. – on which its masked actors can improvise. This approach was borrowed by Fellini when he created the character of Gelsomina, who is also clearly inspired by Charlie Chaplin's 'archetypal' tramp persona.

15. Guido Aristarco (1918–96), editor of the magazine *Cinema Nuovo*, was the leading figure in Italian Marxist criticism. As an opponent of André Bazin's theories, he championed realism based on the analysis of social events and was hostile to any spiritual vision of the world.

16. André Bazin, 'Cabiria ou le voyage au bout du néoréalisme'.

17. The incomprehension that greeted *The Swindle* at the 1955 Venice Film Festival obliged Fellini to cut twenty minutes. In the summer of 2002 the Cinema Ritrovato festival in Bologna showed the version originally screened in Venice.

18. François Truffaut, 'Le Festival de Venise 1955', *Cahiers du cinéma*, 51 (October 1955).

19. In the opening sequences of *L'Avventura*, a character disappears, but the narrative takes no interest in her whereabouts. The film stands today as the work that opened the way to a modern cinema focusing on the inner world rather than the social context.

20. Pascal Bonitzer, 'La Cité des femmes', *Cahiers du cinéma*, 318 (December 1980).

21. Federico Fellini, *Fare un film*.

22. The four episodes of *Boccaccio '70* were directed, respectively, by Vittorio De Sica, Federico Fellini, Mario Monicelli and Luchino Visconti. Each director had to come up with an erotic story along the lines of Boccaccio's *Decameron*.

23. The title *8½* refers to the number of films made by Fellini up to that point and indicates the reflective nature of a film intended as a kind of settling of accounts with himself.

24. *La mia Rimini* is a short autobiographical text. It was subsequently included in Fellini's book *Fare un film*.

25. *Spirits of the Dead* (1968) was an anthology film comprising adaptations of texts by Edgar Allan Poe and directed by Louis Malle, Roger Vadim and Federico Fellini.

26. *Fellini: A Director's Notebook* was produced by NBC.

27. The Expressionist aesthetic of this film turns its form into a projection of Fellini's inner world. The way in which Fellini's interior multiplicity is materially embodied in the sets and direction echoes the Expressionist conception of art.

28. The term 'black aristocracy' denotes murky aristocratic networks close to the power structure of the Vatican. Fellini mocks them directly in the scene featuring the ecclesiastical fashion show.

29. The word *amarcord*, which evokes the expression 'io mi ricordo' (I remember), is a neologism coined by Fellini, after scribbling it on a napkin in an act of automatic writing.

30. Tullio Kezich, *Fellini*, p. 48.

31. In *Le città invisibili* (*Invisible Cities*, 1972), Italo Calvino describes fifty-five imaginary cities with female names. They form a veritable mental world, as none of them has any link with reality, and space and time are totally abstract.

32. Pilar Pedraza, Juan López Gandía, *Federico Fellini*, Cátedra, Madrid, 1993, p. 285.

33. Fellini visited Simenon in Lausanne in 1977 and *L'Express* published a conversation between the two about *Casanova*. This was the start of an unusual friendship. Fellini saw Simenon as a new Casanova. (See Federico Fellini and Georges Simenon, *Carissimo Simenon. Mon cher Fellini*, Cahiers du cinéma, Paris, 1998.)

34. Youssef Ishaghpour, *Opéra et théâtre dans le cinéma d'aujourd'hui*, La Différence, Paris, 1995, p. 12.

35. In the Middle Ages, mad people were chased out of towns and abandoned to their fate, giving rise to the Germanic myth of the ship of fools, *das Narrenschiff*, which was sailing towards the land of the fools, Narragonia. Hieronymus Bosch produced a series of paintings inspired by this myth but all that remains today is a single panel in the Louvre, Paris.

36. Jean Baudrillard, *The Perfect Crime* (1995), Verso, New York, 2008.

37. After discovering Kafka in 1941, Fellini was tempted on several occasions to adapt his work for the screen. He finally decided to include *Amerika* in Fellini's *Intervista* after reading, in *Le Messager européen* (no. 1, May 1987), an article by Milan Kundera noting the existence of 'a great current (probably the most important one) of modern art running from Kafka to Fellini, which, instead of exalting the modern world (like Mayakovsky and Léger), portrays it cynically and penetratingly'.

Sources

Collection Cahiers du cinéma: inside front cover–p.1, pp.2–3, 4–5, 7, 12, 13, 17, 24, 28, 29, 30, 31, 32–3, 34–5, 48–9, 51, 72, 82–3, 84, 93, 96 (4th col.), 98 (2nd col. bottom), 100 (1st col. centre), 103. Collection CAT'S: pp.22, 45 (bottom), 50, 55, 58–9, 63, 64–5, 68–9, 78–9, 85, 86–7, 90–1, 94–5, 104–inside back cover. Collection Cinémathèque française: pp.6, 10, 11, 14, 16, 18–9, 20–1, 26–7, 38–9, 40, 44, 45 (top), 46, 47, 54, 56, 57, 60–1, 62, 66, 67, 70–1, 77, 80, 81, 92, 96 (3rd col.), 97 (2nd col.). Collection Photo12: pp.52–3. Rue des Archives: cover. Screen grabs: pp. 76, 89.

Credits

© Ajosha Prod/Cinecitta: pp.90–1.
© All rights reserved: pp.4–5, 6, 7, 10, 13, 18–9, 81, 96 (1st col.), 97 (2nd col.), 103.
© Archives du 7ᵉ art: pp.52–3.
© BCA: Cover
© Carlo Ponti-De Laurentis: pp.24, 26–7.
© Cinemateca comunale di Bologna: p.97 (1st col.).
© Cineriz: p.55.
© Cineriz/Pathé Consortium Cinéma: p.45 (bottom).
© Courtesy of Warner Bros. Pictures/ PECF: pp.66, 68–9.
© Courtesy of Warner Bros. Pictures/ Pierluigi/Cineteca comunale di Bologna/ PECF: pp.67, 70–1.
© Dino de Laurentiis/Les Films Marceau: pp.14, 30, 32–3, 34–5, 45 (top), 96 (3rd col.).
© Diogenes Verlag A.G. Zurich: pp.42–3.
© Enrica Salfari/Cecchi Gori Group Tiger Cinematografica/ Films A2/La Sept Cinéma/ Cinémax/ Rai Uno Radiotelevisione Italiana: pp.92, 93, 94–5.

© Federico Fellini: p.8.
© France 3 Cinéma/Les Films Ariane, Produzioni Europee Associati (PEA)/Radiotelevisione Italiana/Revcom Films/Stella Films: p.100 (1st col. centre).
© G.B. Paletto: pp.28, 29, 31, 98 (2nd col. bottom).
© Ital-Noleggio Cinematografico: pp.63, 64–5.
© Italy's news photos/Cineteca comunale di Bologna: p.23.
© Laurent Montlau/Aljosha/Cinecittà/ Rai Uno Radiotelevisione Italiana/Fernlyn: pp.72, 89 (4th col. bottom).
© Les Films Marceau/Produzioni Europee: p.56.
© Les Productions Artistes Associés/ Produzioni Europee Associati/ Ultra Film: pp.57, 62.
© Organizzazione Film Internazionale: p.11.
© Osvaldo Civirani: pp.16, 17.
© Paul Ronald: inside front cover–p.1, pp.44 (1st col.), 46, 47, 48–9, 50, 51, 96 (4th col.).

© PEA (Produzioni Europee Associati): pp.58–9.
© PEA / Istituto Luce: pp.85, 86–7.
© Pierluigi/Cineteca Comunale di Bologna: pp.2, 36, 38, 40, 44 (2nd col. top), 44 (2nd col. bottom).
© Photo Studio Cattarinich: p.77.
© Produzioni Europee Associati: pp.74–5.
© RAI/Radiotelevisione Italiana: pp.54, 60–1.
© RAI/Vides Produzione: pp.104–inside back cover.
© Revue 420: p.9.
© RKO Radio Picture Radio/Keith/ Orpheum: pp.20–1, 22.
© Tazio Secchiaroli/Gaumont/Praturion, Pierluigi: pp.78–9.
© The Associated Press: p.80.
© Vides Cinematografica/Radiotelevisione Italiana/Société des Etablissements L. Gaumont/Films A2/Società Investimenti Milanese (S. I. M): pp.82–3, 84.

All reasonable efforts have been made to trace the copyright holders of the photographs used in this book. We apologize to anyone that we were unable to reach.

Opposite page: Federico Fellini in the 1960s.
Cover: Anita Ekberg in *La Dolce Vita* (1960).
Inside front cover: Marcello Mastroianni in *8½* (1963).
Inside back cover: *And the Ship Sails On* (1983).

WITHDRAWN

Cahiers du cinéma Sarl
65, rue Montmartre
75002 Paris

www.cahiersducinema.com

Revised edition © 2011 Cahiers du cinéma Sarl
First published in French as *Federico Fellini* © 2007 Cahiers du cinéma Sarl

ISBN 978 2 8664 2607 1

A CIP catalogue record of this book is available from the British Library.
Series conceived by Claudine Paquot
Concept designed by Werner Jeker/Les Ateliers du Nord
Designed by Pascaline Richir
Translated by Matthew Clarke in association with
First Edition Translations Ltd, Cambridge, UK
Printed in China

This book is due for return on or before the last date shown below.